Young People and Heroin

An Examination of Heroin Use in the North of England

A Report to the Health Education Council

by
Geoffrey Pearson
Mark Gilman
Shirley McIver

Gower

Published by
Gower Publishing Company Limited
Gower House
Croft Road
Aldershot
Hants GU11 3HR
England

Gower Publishing Company
Old Post Road
Brookfield
Vermont 05036
USA

for the
Health Education Council,
78 New Oxford Street,
London W1

ISBN 0 566 05388 8

Printed by Dotesios (Printers) Ltd, Bradford-on-Avon, Wiltshire

CONTENTS

INTRODUCTION AND ACKNOWLEDGEMENTS

This report is based upon a six-month period of fieldwork that was undertaken during the spring and summer months of 1985, funded by the Health Education Council. The research project was conceived on a short timescale in order to be able to offer some preliminary indications of a fluid and rapidly changing social problem.

The fieldwork phase of the project was carried out while I was employed as Reader in Applied Social Studies at the University of Bradford, and it was conducted under my direction by Mr Mark Gilman and Dr Shirley McIver. Mrs Susan Noble acted as Secretary to the research project. We received the unfailing support of Dr Deryck Lambert and Peter Linthwaite from the Health Education Council throughout the project, and Dr Nigel South of the Institute for the Study of Drug Dependence was an invaluable member of our Research Advisory Group.

The need to maintain confidentiality means that we cannot acknowledge by name all those people who gave us their time in order to make this project possible. These include the personnel of numerous public agencies, voluntary bodies, community groups and parents' groups, together with heroin users, ex-users and their families. We are nevertheless indebted to their commitment and insight.

Geoffrey Pearson
Professor of Social Work
Middlesex Polytechnic
November 1985

1 BACKGROUND TO THE PROJECT AND METHODS OF INVESTIGATION

Heroin use in the North of England is a problem of quite recent onset as a matter for serious concern, and it is also a problem that appears to be quite fluid and changeable at the moment. This research project had been designed accordingly as a short six-month fieldwork investigation with very few methodological pretensions, in order to be able to report quickly on two main questions. First, how this apparently novel pattern of heroin use was establishing itself across the North of England; secondly, how the policies and practices of public agencies and voluntary bodies, including various drug liaison initiatives, were responding to this problem.

A further consideration was that the project should assume a neighbourhood focus as one of its objectives. The background to the project's conception was that the project director had been engaged since 1979 in a staff development programme on 'Neighbourhood and Community Involvement' under the auspices of the Northern Regional Staff Development Office of the Probation Service. This programme, which had drawn together practical experiences in some 150 different localities over six years of work, had demonstrated the importance of taking a localised approach to a variety of personal and social problems. These problems tend to manifest themselves quite differently in different neighbourhoods, and there are also quite different patterns of local resources which might be drawn upon in various practical initiatives. This staff development programme also began to highlight in 1983 and early 1984 that heroin misuse was becoming a potentially serious problem in some working-class neighbourhoods in the North of England where previously it had been quite unknown. All the indications were, however, that it was a very localised phenomenon which required a localised research focus.

A draft research proposal had been formulated along these lines by April 1984, and on the basis of subsequent discussions and a re-drafting of the proposal, funding for the research project was eventually secured from the Health Education Council in November 1984. The research fieldwork was conducted during a period of intense publicity on drug issues, including the government anti-heroin campaign of the spring and summer months of 1985.

Preliminary Phase: Agency Contacts

A wide variety of contacts was established in the course of the research, with various public and professional agencies, with voluntary bodies and community groups, with parents' groups and drug liaison initiatives, and with heroin users and ex-users themselves. Our aims in establishing these contacts were twofold: (i) to gain a more coherent understanding than otherwise available of the nature and scale of heroin use among young people; (ii) to explore how the problem of heroin misuse was making itself felt among those groups of professional and voluntary workers whose work brings them into close contact with young people.

These contacts were made by a variety of methods. In the initial phase of the research a circular was distributed to key agencies and voluntary bodies across the Northern region, including Education Departments, community health services, the youth service, Social Services Departments, the Probation Service and the police. This circular set out the aims of our project and asked four broad questions: (i) whether heroin use was considered to be a problem in the area; (ii) whether the problem was more severe in any particular neighbourhood or locality; (iii) whether the agency concerned had deployed any staff to deal specifically with drug issues; and (iv) whether there were any available documents or reports from the agency which might assist our project.

The response to this postal circular was extremely good, although it would be difficult to quantify as a 'response rate' because the agencies concerned sometimes organised their responses differently. For example, for the probation service both the central administrative unit and local area teams were circulated. In some regions the area teams responded independently, whereas in others, local responses were collated by the central administration into a single reply on behalf of the whole region. Nevertheless, in spite of these different patterns of response the replies to the postal circular enabled the research team to make a preliminary mapping of how the heroin problem was manifesting itself across the North of England, in such a way as to show wide local and regional variations which are described in the body of the report.

Concurrently with the postal survey the research staff made personal contacts with agency personnel in each area, and follow-up visits were arranged where appropriate. These were not appropriate in every case, because some agencies (such as education departments and health visitors) made it clear that they had little contact with or knowledge of heroin use and heroin users. Contacts were also made through these channels with a variety of drug liaison committees, self-help groups, parent groups and community support groups. Research staff also began to put out 'feelers' in these preliminary enquiries about known or suspected heroin users and ex-users who would be prepared to talk with us and discuss their problems and experiences, although a more detailed pursuit of the experiences of heroin users was delayed until the second phase of the project.

This first phase of work, including both the collation of incoming information from the postal circular and visits to each area in order to meet individuals and groups from different agencies and voluntary bodies, took 11 weeks to complete, and in all the research staff arranged contacts with 180 individuals and groups in this period. In this early phase it was not always possible, nor even desirable, to sustain a focus solely on heroin use. This was because in many areas we were informed that heroin use was virtually unknown, or that the pattern and scale of heroin misuse had not changed appreciably over recent years. The most significant drug problems in many of these areas were concerned with alcohol, solvents or amphetamines. Among adolescents it was especially true that solvents were seen as a major drug problem, although it is in the nature of solvent misuse that it visits schools and neighbourhoods in epidemic fits and starts, so that at any one time the overall regional picture is very patchy. In a smaller number of areas the use of amphetamine sulphate (known either as 'speed' or 'whizz') was seen as a growing problem among older adolescents. In other areas, particularly in the North-East of England, alcohol abuse was defined as the outstanding drug problem. Cannabis use was also acknowledged to be almost universally widespread, although it was not associated with

2

any major problems.

In spite of the fact that our brief was to study heroin use, it was important to listen to this 'negative evidence' of other forms of drug use, if only because it showed how drug problems — and hence viable forms of health education and service delivery — exhibit wide local and regional variations. These variations, together with possible ways of understanding them, are described in the main body of the research report.

Local Studies

On the basis of the work described so far, the research team were able to build up a preliminary mapping of how heroin use is distributed across the North of England, and the ways in which the problem was making an impact on the routine work of different agencies. We were also able to identify a small number of areas for more detailed research at a neighbourhood level.

In deciding upon which neighbourhoods to study more closely there were a number of considerations. Most obviously, those areas which did not appear to have a significant heroin problem at the moment were excluded from further study. A small number of other areas were excluded on the grounds that major research had either been recently undertaken there or was already underway. For example, there had been a recent drug indicator survey in South Tyneside which had established a low prevalence, and which had itself been transferred from its original location in Cleveland where problem drug users had been found to form only a negligible proportion of the population. By contrast, although it was known that there was a serious heroin problem in the Wirral area of Merseyside, research was already being undertaken there by Parker's team from Liverpool University. There was also a prevalence study underway in Leeds, conducted by Tober from the Leeds Addiction Unit.

The localities which were chosen for more detailed study fell into two groups: (i) those where it was known, from our independent investigations, that there was a well-established heroin network; (ii) localities where, although we did not have any independent evidence of a widespread pattern of heroin use, it was rumoured by professionals in the area that heroin use was to be found.

The precise locations of the neighbourhoods which were chosen for detailed study have been disguised within the research report on the grounds of confidentiality. Nevertheless, it is possible to say that they were in Greater Manchester, Humberside, Merseyside, South Yorkshire and West Yorkshire. In each case, extended discussions took place with local agency personnel in terms of how heroin-related problems were making an impact upon their routine work, as well as with numbers of drug users in each locality. Local residents associations and other interested parties were also contacted.

Other forms of information were collected on each neighbourhood including data held by local authority housing departments and planning departments. The Small Area Statistics of the 1981 Census were also analysed at Enumeration District level for those neighbourhoods which exhibited a serious problem of heroin use, with a particular focus on the age structure of the population, levels of unemployment at a local level, the proportions of single-parent families and other relevant social indicators. A brief summary of these Census materials is contained in Appendix I, 'Heroin and Unemployment: A Neighbourhood Analysis of the 1981 Census Small Area Statistics', which shows how heroin misuse and social deprivation tend to gather together in tight geographical proximity.

3

Self-Help Groups and Heroin-User Contacts

In addition to this neighbourhood-based work in the second phase of the project, contact was made with a number of parents' groups, self-help groups and drug liaison initiatives. The location of these groups did not always correspond to the neighbourhoods which had been chosen for detailed study, for the simple reason that not all of these neighbourhoods had developed active community support networks. It was our view that although this involved some relaxation of our neighbourhood focus, it was nevertheless important to learn something from the experiences of these kinds of voluntary initiative, wherever they might be located. Contacts were made with groups of this kind in Cumbria, Greater Manchester, Humberside, Merseyside, North-East Lancashire, North Yorkshire, West Yorkshire, and elsewhere. A number of these groups had a multi-drug focus, whereas others were largely focused on opiate misuse. As well as interviewing individual group members, the research staff also attended group meetings where this was permitted and appropriate.

Finally, the research staff made contact with heroin users and ex-users in this second phase of the project, for the purpose of in-depth interviews and group discussions. These people were often introduced to us by the staff of various agencies initially, although heroin users and ex-users also introduced research staff to friends and acquaintances who were prepared to be interviewed. Because of the short life of the project we were not able to pursue this 'snowballing' activity to its fullest effect, which is undoubtedly considerable. In one instance a young man, having heard about our project from a heroin-using friend whom we had interviewed, even went so far as to contact the research team on his own initiative in order to offer his services. In other cases people were happy to gather together a small group of friends or relatives in order to talk with the research staff, although not everyone was happy to have these discussions tape-recorded. Other people, of course, flatly refused to have anything to do with us or with our project.

During this second phase of the research a total of 168 contacts were made with professional and voluntary agencies, involving further follow-up visits and discussions where appropriate. Interviews and discussions took place with 67 heroin users and ex-users, of whom 42 were interviewed individually, while 29 were interviewed in-depth, generating 20 hours of transcribable tape-recordings and many thousands of words of field notes. A small number of ex-users were also contacted who now worked for drug agencies and voluntary bodies, although the focus for these contacts was their work with drug users and not their own experiences with drugs. More than 30 drug liaison initiatives and parents' groups were identified, together with more which were either in the planning stage or had become extinct, and seven parents' groups and self-help groups participated in our research. Fieldwork was brought to a conclusion in September 1985, and this report was submitted to the Health Education Council in November 1985. It is hoped that at some future date it will be possible to arrange some feedback meetings with interested parties.

2 THE GROWTH AND DIVERSITY OF THE HEROIN PROBLEM

Heroin use in the North of England is at the moment an extremely scattered and localised phenomenon. In some towns and cities there are pockets of quite serious heroin misuse, which in a small number of cases can be properly regarded as having reached 'epidemic' proportions. By contrast, in other areas the heroin problem is much less significant, and sometimes even almost unknown. It is important at the outset, therefore, to give some indication of this enormous local and regional variation, together with a brief overview of the growth of heroin misuse in recent years.

Without question one of the most striking findings of our research is the way in which heroin use is distributed quite differently to the east and west of the Pennines. In the east there is much less of a problem with heroin at the moment, which is not to say that there is no problem at all. Nor that to the east of the Pennines one does not find small pockets of serious heroin misuse in some towns and cities. Nevertheless, the problem is much more extensive to the west of the Pennines where it is not only restricted to the large urban conurbations of Manchester and Merseyside, in that it is also found in some of the towns and valleys of North-East Lancashire, in Carlisle, and elsewhere.

A further aspect of this diversity is that even in a town or city which has a well-established heroin problem, there is an uneven development so that not all neighbourhoods will be affected in the same way, if at all. A survey of drug misuse on housing estates in North London has recently found a similarly diverse pattern, with heroin use concentrated in some localities and not others, even though these might be in close proximity to each other (O'Bryan, 1985).

There are also variations in patterns and styles of heroin use, most distinctively around whether the drug is injected as in the 'traditional' style of Britain's heroin addicts of the 1960s and 1970s who were almost entirely centred in London as any visible presence, or whether the drug is smoked or inhaled in a variety of ways — known in different districts by a number of terms such as 'tooting', 'snorting', 'chasing the dragon', or simply 'chasing', 'dragoning' and 'tasting'.

This pattern of local and regional diversity reflects a wider pattern of variation across the British Isles as a whole. In all probability London remains the centre of gravity of opiate use, although in recent months most publicity has been directed towards Merseyside, which has been dubbed 'Smack City' in the popular press. In Scotland the heroin problem in Glasgow, first highlighted by Ditton and Speirits (1981), has been widely acknowledged, and more recently Edinburgh has experienced its own serious difficulties. And whereas Dublin has suffered a major heroin problem, Belfast apparently has not.

If there is no uniform pattern to the extent of heroin use, there are also wide variations in the responses of control agencies. Different styles of policing are evident in different areas, and drugs liaison initiatives have assumed different forms in different places. There are also variations in the medical response, particularly whether methadone maintenance is available from the local drug dependency unit. In some areas methadone is available to those who refer themselves for treatment. In other places it is not, and local medical practice adheres to a strict 'abstinence' model in treatment and rehabilitation programmes. These kinds of variation make it impossible to offer generalised advice to heroin users and their families in terms of what kind of help is available to them, or how they should seek it.

Over and against this diversity, there is a general agreement across the North of England that there was a substantial shift in the heroin problem between 1979 and 1981 when the drug became more easily available and at a much reduced price at street level, because of the influx of 'brown' heroin which had its source in Iran and a short time later in Pakistan. This shift of emphasis was also noted at around the same time in London where it corresponded with the emergence of a previously unknown type of heroin user — young men from working-class council estates (Dorn and South, 1985). Prior to this the major site for heroin abuse in London had for many years centred on the West End 'scene' of Piccadilly and its environs, or in bohemian-style enclaves such as Notting Hill. It is also often asserted, although this is much more difficult to substantiate, that the influx of cheap and plentiful heroin was followed by a sharp drop in the age of the typical heroin user. We shall examine this evidence in more detail later in this report.

Alongside these general trends, a major difference between London and the North of England is that prior to the influx of 'brown' heroin between 1979 and 1981, there had been no tradition of extensive heroin misuse in the Northern cities. There had, of course, been scattered pockets of opiate use in various Northern towns and cities prior to this, but nothing compared to the scale that is now encountered in some localities. As a consequence, there was also a corresponding lack of experience of heroin abuse among relevant professional groups and also among the police in the North. This lack of experience continues to have important consequences for service delivery and health education. Moreover, in some areas the situation has continued to change since the early 1980s, and in some districts it is felt that there has been an even more rapid acceleration of the heroin problem within the past two years, or even more recently than that. In fact, the heroin scene is extremely fluid at the moment, and many of the facts which we have established in our research may well be subject to further change in the coming years, if not months.

A survey conducted in three Yorkshire cities in 1979 by a staff member of the London Hungerford Project offers a useful snapshot of existing patterns of drug misuse at the time when 'brown' heroin first became available (Fox, 1979). In Bradford, to take one example, two main groups of drug users could be identified. The first group consisted mainly of young men, with an average age of 18 years, who were unemployed and living in rented accommodation. Their drug misuse consisted of a combination of barbiturates, amphetamines and alcohol. (For an account of a different style of poly-drug use in London at a similar point in time, see Jamieson et al., 1984.) The second group in Bradford were considerably older, average age 28 years, and their preferred drug was dipipanone, an opiate marketed under the name of 'Diconal' and available at that time on prescription. The report also noted that Iranian 'brown' heroin had become available in recent months, at the absurdly low street price of £35–£40 per gramme, compared with £80–£100 in London at that time. The novelty of this situation is reflected in Fox's observation that, 'Most people felt that cheap heroin was just a flash in the pan.'

The sudden appearance of cheap and plentiful heroin did not change people's drug preferences overnight. Indeed, for many established opiate-users Diconal ('dikes',

6

'dikeys' or 'pinkies') remained the drug of choice until quite recently when it was taken off the list of prescribed drugs. Even during our fieldwork in 1985 we spoke with opiate-users who mourned the fact that they could no longer obtain 'dikes', and who considered heroin to be a far inferior drug, although this was not a universal judgement. In a few instances we even encountered opiate users who had become abstinent when Diconal was no longer available. One reason for these continuing drug preferences was that Diconal contains an anti-emetic substance (cyclizine) which could overcome the nausea commonly induced by opiates, which was one of the drug's original marketing attractions (cf. ABPI, 1974, p. 747).

Nevertheless, the availability of cheap heroin in the North of England during the early 1980s signalled a truly qualitative shift in many towns and cities where heroin had been previously almost unknown. This novel situation also coincided precisely with the sharp increase of unemployment in the Northern region, so that this coincidence cemented relationships between heroin use and unemployment levels in some localities, whatever the mechanism of these relationships might be. In a major study from the 1960s of heroin use among juveniles in New York, it was noted that those neighbourhoods where heroin use was most prevalent were economically deprived areas which were also characterised by a sense of futility that was conducive to narcotics experimentation (Chein *et al.*, 1964). Within our own research an analysis of the Small Area Statistics of the 1981 Census has revealed a correspondence between the extent and distribution of heroin use and other signs of social deprivation in a number of localities. We shall describe these findings in Appendix I.

In summary, we can say that although the sharp increase of heroin use was reflected across the Northern region — as indicated by available measures such as notifications to the Home Office, drug seizures and arrests, persons registered for treatment, etc. — it was nevertheless subject to large local and sub-regional variations, with the most severely affected areas concentrated to the west of the Pennines. This geographical variation is also reflected in the evidence collected together in the government's recent survey of health authorities, *Drug Misuse, Prevalence and Service Provision* (DHSS, 1985) and agreed by all those with a professional interest in the matter whom we contacted in the course of our research, although many of our informants could not understand where the statistical estimates contained in the DHSS report had come from.

It is equally significant that the geographical divide between the east and west of the Pennines is reflected in the distribution of parents' groups and community support groups in the North of England. These have been thrown up in profusion to the west in response to the increased problems of drug abuse and their effects on families and the wider community, but they are very thin on the ground in the east. As we have already indicated, this does not mean that heroin use is unknown in the towns and cities of the east such as Bradford, Hull, Leeds, Sunderland, Newcastle upon Tyne, Huddersfield, Sheffield, Rotherham, Scunthorpe and York. Indeed, there are identifiable areas (such as Rotherham in South Yorkshire) where the extent of heroin misuse is almost certainly more widespread than in some parts of the North-West. Even so, it is the broad geographical diversity of the heroin problem as we have described it which dominates the picture in the North of England.

One can only speculate as to how this diversity has come about. One obvious consideration is to do with the way in which patterns of distribution and supply have evolved over time. This itself is reflected in variations in the street price of heroin in different areas, which can vary from £65 per gramme in some parts of the west to £100 per gramme or even more in some parts of the east, although there is a wide elasticity in the market value for heroin even within a single area. It is also tempting to speculate how cultural and subcultural variations might influence drug choices. It could be that the more cosmopolitan ambience of cities such as Liverpool and Manchester means that the culture of these cities is more open to change and innovation in traditions of drug use, as in other things — although this does not help to explain the extensive heroin problem in Carlisle, Chester, Macclesfield, or the towns and valleys of North-East Lancashire. But however we might choose to explain these geographical variations, they have considerable implications for effective health education which will need to be closely tailored to local needs and problems, if it is to be relevant and effective.

3 HEROIN USERS AND PATTERNS OF USE

If the growth of the heroin problem is characterised by substantial and important variations, then what of the heroin users themselves? Do they conform to a single pattern, in the sense of a typical 'addict personality'? Are they in any way different from earlier generations of heroin users, either in terms of their age or other characteristics? Or is there a typical style of heroin use, in terms of whether the drug is smoked or injected, compared with the dominant pattern of injection in the past?

The 'Normalisation' of Heroin Use

Research has established over many years that heroin addiction is compatible with widely varying lifestyles, from stable addicts with a more or less normal family life and employment record, to those who live a chaotic 'junkie' lifestyle, living by crime and by the daily hustle, with the attendant risks of undernourishment, dirty syringes, overdoses and imprisonment. This enormous variability, which does not accord with the stereotypical view that all heroin users live a 'junkie' lifestyle, had been first elaborated in the work of Stimson (1973), and was confirmed in a major follow-up study over a ten-year period of addicts who were attending London clinics through the 1970s (Stimson and Oppenheimer, 1982).

Nevertheless, it is probably true that a decade ago the 'typical' heroin user would be more likely to have been someone leading a bohemian-type lifestyle, or to have been someone with some form of temperamental instability. However, as the heroin-using population has steadily grown in recent years this has undoubtedly become less true, so that although some individuals are psychologically more vulnerable to opiate misuse, attempts to explain heroin use solely in terms of personality factors and psychopathology are nowadays quite inadequate (cf. Strang, 1984). As Hartnoll (1984) has argued, 'the importance of individual differences is an unknown factor, though a sudden surge in "addictive personalities" is an unlikely explanation of rapid changes in the overall pattern of heroin use and availability'.

In order to reach a better understanding of the changing characteristics of the heroin-using population, it is helpful to think by analogy with the changing characteristics of the unemployed in recent years. Some years ago, during the era of full employment, the unemployed contained a high proportion of people who suffered from various kinds of illness, physical handicap or psychological disability and who were for these reasons marginal to the labour force. However, as the economic recession deepened and

9

increasing numbers of people became unemployed this proportion has decreased sharply, so that the characteristics of the unemployed came to resemble more closely the characteristics of the population as a whole (cf. Hakim, 1982).

It is likely that as the heroin-using population has increased, a similar mechanism has been at work. So that heroin users have increasingly come to resemble the general population, or what one might call 'ordinary people'. This is a change which is often easily recognisable to those with a long-standing connection with the heroin scene, whether as a professional or as a drug user. The shift is here described to us by a man in his early thirties who used heroin for twelve years, both in London and in Yorkshire:

> '*Have the people using heroin changed in your experience, from what you used to see in the sixties and seventies?*'

> 'Oh yes, definitely, there has been a change. I think that people using heroin now are a bit more together, when they start you know. I think the people that used it in the sixties tended to be people like myself, you know, social casualties, that kind of thing .... They're a tougher lot now .... There's no such thing as a "type" either, they're all sort of different ... usually ultra-straight.' (Keith, 32 years, South Yorkshire)

A similar observation was offered to us from another experienced ex-user, this time from the other side of the Pennines:

> 'Oh you know how it was, like. You used to be able to tell 'em a mile off, well you used to be able to ... typical junkies, you know, scars up their arms, clapped-out hippies, that kind of thing, the whole works ... you know what I mean .... But now, well, I don't know about you, but I couldn't tell one if I fell over him in the street.' (Alan 24 years, Manchester)

The Decreasing Age of Heroin Users

If heroin users are more likely to be 'ordinary' people than they were ten years ago, then a particularly vexed question is whether they are also significantly more youthful. And we describe this as a vexed question because although most of the publicity in recent months has been about young heroin users, who are even in their early teens, the vast bulk of professional experience indicates a significantly older age structure than this, which is also reflected in official statistics. Indeed, nearly all of our informants — whether professionals or heroin users — either discounted the existence of very young addicts, or described them as highly exceptional.

The background to this controversy is easily sketched in. The age-structure of the opiate-using population that was inherited from the late 1960s and early 1970s, as indicated by a variety of sources, tended to be people in their mid to late twenties or early thirties. The sample of registered addicts studied by Stimson and Oppenheimer (1982), for example, had an average age of 25 years at the start of the research in 1969. Ten years later, a study by the City Roads crisis intervention unit which had been established to cater for young poly-drug users with chaotic lifestyles (who were predominantly injecting barbiturates, although they were also experienced in opiates) showed that more than half of the people who used this facility between 1978 and 1981 were over 25 years of age (Jamieson *et al.*, 1984). It was noted, however, that the female clientele of City Roads tended to be younger than the men: whereas only one tenth of the men were under twenty years of age, one third of the women fell into this age category. This broad age-structure was also reflected throughout the 1970s in Home Office statistics on new notifications, with the proportion of new addicts under twenty-one years of age dropping steadily during

10

the 1970s. However, this trend was reversed in the 1980s thus lending some statistical support to the view that heroin addicts have been getting younger in recent years (cf. Hartnoll, 1984).

It is necessary to read certain adjustments into these figures, however, because in common with other forms of official statistics they might contain various kinds of subtle biases and misrepresentations. It can be said with confidence, for example, that official measures — whether these are centrally collected statistics, or records of people entering treatment — will tend to de-emphasise the youthfulness of the actual drug-using population. This is because it will invariably take some time for a heroin user to come to the notice of public authorities. In the early stages of a heroin-using career, a person's drug use is often not a problem to them, so that it might take several years before a heroin user discovers the motivation to seek help, or before he or she comes to the attention of the courts because of drug-related crime. Very little is known about the 'dark figure' of heroin use, and those people who are in the early stages of opiate use — commonly known as 'experimental' or 'recreational' users — are particularly elusive. The paucity of research on 'recreational' opiate use is partly explained by the difficulties of gaining access to this type of user before they might come to official notice, but also possibly by ethical considerations whereby investigators fear 'that if they reported the existence of occasional users they might be accused of endorsing experimentation with opiates' (Zinberg, 1984, p. 243).

It is a reasonable guess, then, that the 'dark figure' will consist of a younger population of heroin users than those who have come to public notice. Even so, this view must be balanced against a counter-argument that heroin users will nowadays tend to come to public notice more quickly than they did through the 1970s. The fact that the new type of heroin user is more like the population at large, and also more likely to be a member of an intact family structure unlike the earlier generation of 'bohemian' and 'bedsit' users, means that he or she might be more likely to seek help earlier in their heroin-using careers than formerly (cf. Strang, 1984). It is also a possibility that heroin users will come to the attention of the law more quickly than in the past: in one area of Liverpool, for example, we were told by informants that heroin users in their late teens were proving to be both inexperienced and incompetent petty thieves who easily fell into the hands of the police. One added possibility is that, in the absence of a well-informed drug culture which could offer cautionary advice to the novice user by which he or she might sustain a pattern of non-addictive 'recreational' use over time, heroin users pass more quickly through the 'experimental' stage of use into compulsive use and thereby become more quickly addicted.

It is simply not possible to sift the available evidence in such a way that might offer a clear-cut answer to the question of whether the average age of the heroin user has sharply decreased in recent years. Our own informants offered a variety of indications of the 'typical' age of a heroin user in their own localities, and in many cases their experience tended to confirm the view that the age profile of heroin abuse is not substantially different from what it was throughout the 1970s. However, it is necessary to treat this evidence from various professional sources with some caution. It offers only a very partial kind of knowledge to learn, for example, that in West Yorkshire the average age of people convicted for heroin offences in the past year was 30 years of age. It is equally a partial kind of knowledge that the typical problem presenting to the probation service in one part of Manchester was said to be an ex-addict or user in his late twenties or early thirties, or, from the same region, that a recent analysis of drug addicts on a clinic waiting list showed them to have an average age of 28 years (Watson, 1985).

Estimates such as these only offer a partial knowledge of what the 'typical' heroin user might be like, for the simple reason that different agencies will tend to have different kinds of 'typical' clientele. So, in one locality of Merseyside with a highly visible heroin

11

problem of worrying dimensions, the 'typical' heroin user seen by a probation officer is a young man in his late teens or early twenties. Whereas in the same locality, a 'typical' heroin case presenting to the Social Services Department would be a single parent in her early to mid-twenties. And finally, the local Intermediate Treatment unit which did most of its work with groups of young offenders aged 14–16 years had recently become aware that a significant proportion of the agency's clientele had experimented with a variety of drugs, including not only alcohol and solvents, but also heroin.

What we can say is that these different estimates of the 'typical' age of a heroin user presenting to different agencies in different places indicate the complexities of the heroin problem, and that the age structure of the heroin-using population is one further aspect of the diversity of heroin users and heroin-related problems. There is no such thing as *the* heroin problem, and these different estimates indicate different dimensions of a multifaceted phenomenon. They also represent different target audiences for health education, as well as for treatment and rehabilitation, whose needs will be vastly different and who are only likely to be encouraged into safer avenues of drug choice by different lines of persuasive invitation.

Finally, what can be said about the widespread publicity which has been given in recent months to very young heroin users in their early teens? Our research suggests that a vastly disproportionate amount of attention has been given to this problem, and that as far as school-age youngsters are concerned, solvent abuse continues to be the major drug choice in most areas. Education departments indicated in response to our postal circular, almost without exception, that heroin use was not considered to be any kind of problem in the schools. In some parts of Merseyside there is real concern about heroin users in the younger age group, although on all the available evidence it does seem that Merseyside represents quite a unique form of heroin problem at the present time. More generally, there is a very real danger that given the high public profile of heroin misuse, it could be forgotten that the forms of drug misuse most commonly encountered by youth workers and others who work with the younger age group relate to alcohol and solvent abuse.

If professional opinion tended to discount the problem of the very young heroin user as merely exceptional, the views of heroin users themselves were even more emphatic. Sometimes this amounted to no more than a blunt denial:

'No, there's no young 'uns involved. Kids are still kids round here.' (Cheryl, 21 years, South Yorkshire)

'Oh, they wouldn't sell it to kids.. phhh . . . it's out of the question. I've never, ever actually seen young kids buying it.' (Eddie, 21 years, Merseyside)

Other people offered slightly more elaborated justifications for their view:

'No, everyone round here who's at it, they're all over 18, in their 20s, older than that too. There just isn't no kids on it, and that's that. All right, some of these on it now, they'll tell you they started on it when they were 13 and all that. But they didn't. It's all talk. They think they get status, that kind of thing, you know. If someone says, "I started on it when I were twelve, thirteen", that kind of thing . . . they never even saw it, know what I mean, until they were . . . oh I don't know, much older than that. In any case, no one'd sell it to them, either, even if they wanted it.'

'*Why not?*'

'Why not? Because it's just wrong . . . out of order . . . you know.' (Kevin, 23 years, Manchester)

'Like I said, I've been around the smack scene a long time. Not just here but all over the place, and I've never come across any of these free samples you hear about ... chance'd be a fine thing! And as for the young ones, well ... they haven't got the money have they? Where are they gonna get the money from to buy smack, regular like? You hear all this stuff in the papers. That 14-year-old lad in Liverpool what died, that kind of thing. It's sad, all right. It's sad. But they're giving the wrong impression, as if it was all the young ones. I've known ... I don't know ... maybe one or two 15 or 16 year olds at it. I've heard of that down in London. But it's the exception. It really is, believe me.' (Gary, 27 years, Humberside)

Finally, in justifying their view of the non-involvement of school-age children in the heroin scene, some heroin users described this in terms of a morality within the heroin network which sometimes touched upon wider loyalties of family and kinship:

'You hear a lot about people selling it at school gates. Do you find that ever?'

'No, I don't think that's true. It never happens round here .... There is, like, sort of rules to it. You know what I mean, like, sort of rules to getting involved in the whole smack scene. You don't sell it to kids. And you don't like even give any to a kid .... People have got, there's still a bit of self-respect involved .... It's not completely out of hand. There's sort of, like, rules and do's and don't sort of thing.' (Jack, 22 years, Merseyside)

'If people stood dealing outside school gates, I reckon they'd get battered for it. Their big brothers'd come up and everything. I reckon I'd punch someone myself, like, selling outside the gates. I would. Giving it to kids, like, it's only gonna mean one thing isn't it? Old women getting mugged and all that .... 'Cos little kids, like, they're too scared to do some things [i.e. shoplifting or house-breaking] but they'd mug an old woman and all that like, cos it's easy. That's why I wouldn't like the kids to get on it.'

'Is there much violence involved?'

'No, not really, not that way like .... I know one lad that mugged a woman. He got battered everywhere ... a real outcast, like. No one'd sell him smack or nothing.' (John, 19 years, Merseyside)

The existence of a morality in the lower reaches of the heroin economy is invariably discounted in sensational news stories about the 'evil pushers'. But it exists, nevertheless, and also extends to the commonly expressed view among heroin users that it is wrong for people who do not use heroin themselves to supply it — something which was also found in a recent study of the illicit heroin market in London (cf. Lewis *et al.*, 1985).

As far as the young user is concerned, this morality is an active disincentive to supplying young people with heroin, and it reinforces the view that the problem of the young adolescent heroin user has been overplayed in the news media. Nevertheless, in common with other moralities, it can sometimes break down. Eddie from Merseyside, who it will be remembered thought that selling heroin to young people was 'out of the question', had encountered young heroin users occasionally. He had 'never actually seen young kids buying it', but he knew that they sometimes got hold of it from somewhere:

'...but like, I've been walking along the street and, like, girls of 14 have said to me, "Have you got a drop of vinegar on you lad?" I mean, for hitting it up in the arm ... it makes you sick.' (Eddie, 21 years, Merseyside)

The young adolescent heroin user may have been overplayed in some recent publicity, but nevertheless he or she is there somewhere, lurking in the shadows of the heroin scene.

Even so, it remains true that the typical heroin user is more likely to be someone in his or her twenties or late teens, and that among the younger age group alcohol and solvents are the forms of drug misuse most likely to be encountered. So that an over-emphasis on the very young user can misrepresent not only the kinds of drug which are more likely to attract (and be available to) the young adolescent, but also what the heroin problem in Britain today is actually about.

Smoking or Injecting: Individual and Cultural Preferences

Finally in this brief overview of the 'typicality' of heroin users, we turn to the question of whether the drug is smoked or injected — something which is once more subject to local and regional variation, over and above merely individual preferences.

It has been widely observed that with the arrival of cheap 'brown' heroin, quite apart from the wider availability and higher quality of heroin in circulation, there were other significant changes. So that whereas the older existing heroin subculture had been centred on injection ('shooting up', 'cranking up', 'hitting it up') a novel aspect of the heroin problem was that it took the form of smoking or inhaling the drug. This is undoubtedly true in many areas, and it is equally true that the realisation that heroin could be smoked removed a major cultural barrier (the taboo against self-injection) which had previously worked against the widespread dispersal of the heroin habit.

There is also a feeling abroad that there is a common progression in the career of a heroin user, whereby someone is initially introduced to the drug through 'chasing' or 'tooting', but eventually changes the mode of administration to injection. Various justifications are offered for this view. Smoking is without question an inefficient mode of use (quantities of the drug, quite literally, 'go up in smoke') and as the user's dependence and tolerance increase, so the economic costs mount. Injection is a more economically-efficient mode of heroin use, so that an addict might find it necessary to cross the injection barrier if his or her habit is to remain financially viable. Another incentive is that the 'rush' from injection is commonly felt to be more intense and pleasurable than from smoking.

There is definitely some truth in these assertions, and we have collected case histories which conform to this pattern. However, this is not at all the universal picture. There are some localities where smoking has remained the dominant mode of administration over quite long periods of time, without any evidence of widespread escalation to injecting, in spite of the fact that individuals and groups had occasionally experimented with injection techniques. In other instances people will begin injecting from the first occasion of heroin use, and we have also come across people with an already established habit of injecting opiates (including heroin, morphine or Diconal) who switched to smoking when 'brown' heroin appeared. In one case this counter-movement may have been because a man's veins were so badly damaged by injecting Diconal (a drug which is not intended for injection) that he found it necessary to smoke. In another instance a woman in her mid-twenties who had been injecting heroin for 18 months started smoking the drug as part of a self-administered 'health education' and 'drug reduction' programme, because she recognised that smoking carried fewer risks (such as overdoses, hepatitis, etc.) than injecting, and in fact she is now abstinent from opiates. In other cases experienced injectors felt that 'brown' heroin probably contained too many impurities for it to be safe to continue injecting, and so they switched to smoking. There is also a further consideration which is that 'brown' heroin from Iran or Pakistan has been specially prepared for smoking, and it must be acidified if it is to be rendered soluble for injection purposes. This seems to be most commonly done by means of a 'Jiff lemon', and one of our informants told us that if heroin prepared in this way is injected and does not

14

connect properly with the vein, then it could give you a very sore arm which acted as a disincentive to injection. In his own case, he had injected opiates for some years (including morphine, illicit pharmaceutically pure heroin, 'Chinese' heroin and Diconal) but had switched to smoking when 'brown' heroin became most easily available, because otherwise it was just 'too much of a hassle'. It is possibly because of the need to acidify 'brown' heroin that 'skin-popping' (intramuscular as opposed to intravenous injection) which is so widely known in North America appears to be a rarity in Britain today.

The technology of drug administration therefore bears upon choices as to whether heroin will be smoked or injected. But it is equally important to recognise that such choices will also reflect already established traditions of drug misuse in any given locality. A crucial factor here is whether there had been an established tradition of injecting amphetamines — that is ,'speed' or 'whizz' as it is increasingly known in some parts of the North of England. Where there had been such a pattern of amphetamine abuse (or barbiturate abuse) prior to the arrival of cheap heroin in the early 1980s, then our evidence suggests that there was a much increased likelihood that people would move immediately on to injecting heroin when the drug became more freely available. This appears to have been the case in Carlisle, where the heroin problem is generally stated to be predominantly an injection scene, and the same pattern is reflected elsewhere. Established patterns of 'poly-drug' use in the 1970s can therefore weigh heavily in determining drug choices in the 1980s with respect to heroin misuse. So that when injection was already a dominant feature of the poly-drug culture, this seemed likely to carry over into heroin use, whereas if the preferred style had involved 'snorting' amphetamine, then it seemed more likely that heroin would be initially smoked or inhaled.

In some areas, the habit of smoking heroin has retained its dominance from the beginning in the early 1980s — this, according to our informants, has been the case in Merseyside — which might be because within the local drug culture there is a residual opposition to crossing the injection barrier. In the drug cultures of the late 1960s and early 1970s, which focused on the use of cannabis and hallucinogens, both heroin and 'junkies' were held in widespread contempt. Amphetamine abuse was also frowned on, and the slogan 'Speed Kills' was widely popularised through the 'underground' press. It is common nowadays to assert that these forms of subcultural opposition towards opiates and injection have been sharply disrupted, although our research suggests that they do still carry weight in some areas. In one neighbourhood of Manchester, for example, we found that local heroin users who 'tooted' the drug were deeply·suspicious of a lone injector in their locality whom they regarded as a sad case who was 'over the top' and 'too far gone'.

Adherence to subcultural values such as these can have a wider application in determining drug choices, going beyond the question of whether heroin will be injected to whether it will be acceptable to use heroin at all. An outright form of opposition to heroin use was described to us in a Liverpool neighbourhood where heroin had appeared some 18 months earlier, but where local youths had applied pressure against heroin users within their peer-group who were described in the local vernacular as 'dick heads' who, if they did not comply with this pressure, were encouraged to move elsewhere. This pressure fell short of the vigilante action widely reported in the national press in August 1985 when sections of the black community in Liverpool 8, or Toxteth, moved against people who were alleged to be heroin dealers. We received several reports of vigilante action against heroin-using networks in a number of localities. During our fieldwork in the summer of 1985 there were also vivid graffiti in Liverpool 8, proclaiming 'This is Toxteth, Not Croxteth: NO SMACK!' A number of informants told us that people trying to buy heroin in Liverpool 8 had been given rough treatment, and in one instance a man who was visiting Leeds from another area had tried to buy heroin in the Chapeltown district where, in his own words, he had been given 'a lecture' advising him against the dangers of heroin. Although cannabis is used widely as a social drug within the Afro-Caribbean community, and more specifically among Rastafarians, there appears to be a determined cultural opposition to the dissemination of heroin.

Forms of cultural opposition such as these could well supply important adjuncts to effective health education strategies at a local level, whether in terms of outright prevention or 'harm-minimisation' strategies directed against more dangerous practices such as injection (cf. ACMD, 1984). However, it is important to recognise how varied and localised these responses can be. In one area of Yorkshire a worker in a drugs agency described to us a group of young men whom he knew, who had regularly smoked cannabis together and who had also taken 'acid' trips. When heroin appeared on the scene they were curious about it, but when they first tried it they found that it was 'too heavy a stone' which did not fit in with their accustomed recreational lifestyle which had revolved around cannabis and hallucinogens. As a consequence they immediately lost interest in heroin and did not carry their experimentation any further. By contrast, from another part of the North, consisting of small towns scattered among moors and farmland, we learned how a group of skinhead youths had made different drug choices. There was a strong cannabis culture in their locality, which according to local gossip had been imported from the South of England by 'ageing hippies' in search of the counter-cultural 'good life' in the early 1970s, who had been attracted to the area by low property values and the availability of cheap smallholdings. Amidst a typical cluster of discontents between these people defined as 'foreigners' and 'off-comers' by those 'born and bred' in the area, the skinheads had taken these arguments one step further by defining the 'soft drug' culture as 'degenerate' because of its association with long hair, beards and faded blue jeans. In the skinhead view of things, 'smack' was a more 'manly' drug, whereas cannabis was for 'wankers'. So their involvement with heroin was defined by a subcultural opposition to what they described as 'clapped-out hippies', 'soft Southerners' and 'hairy fairy vegetarianism'. A rational set of drug choices might well have defined cannabis smoking as less harmful than heroin use, but it is so often the case that drug involvements are inseparable from wider considerations of lifestyle and the subcultural meanings which are attached to particular forms of drug use.

Idiosyncratic variations are therefore possible within different localities which can have important effects in shaping the drug choices of individuals, according to local cultural and subcultural preferences. These influences can shape both generalised patterns of drug use, as well as more specific questions such as whether heroin will be smoked or injected. And it is vitally important to recognise that a major determining influence on whether heroin users will cross the injection barrier is the surrounding drug culture, and not merely individual whim. Where the pre-existing 'poly-drug' culture had embraced injection techniques, then it is common for someone to inject heroin from the first instance of use. In the following case, for example, a married couple in their mid-twenties are discussing how they first got involved in heroin, having been accustomed previously to using amphetamine sulphate on a recreational basis at weekends:

> Linda: 'You see up till then we'd been having, started having a bit of sulphate before then, didn't we?'

> Brian: 'Yeh.'

> Linda: 'And then a friend came round, said I couldn't get nowt, sulphate, so ... got this heroin, and that was it.'

> Brian: 'That was it, that was the start.'

16

Interviewer: 'Did you smoke it then, or . . .'

Brian: 'No I injected it.'

Interviewer: 'Straight away?'

Brian: 'Straight away, 'cos I were injecting speed like first.'

Interviewer: 'Oh right.'

(Linda and Brian, mid-twenties, South Yorkshire)

Here crossing the injection barrier is described to us in casual, matter of fact terms as an issue of little consequence. By contrast, in the following excerpt we find a quite different attitude:

> 'I can't explain it like, you know, like cranking is the extent . . . you know what I mean. Like once you do that you're fucking, you're bad . . . y'know what I mean . . . you're sort of like, it's evil, you know what I mean, most people regard it sort of like that. Once you inject it they think, "Oh fucking hell!" That's the furthest you can ever go like. And the people are, y'know, frightened of doing that, and like they've still got a bit of self respect not to do that.' (Keith, 20 years, Merseyside)

It does not make any sense to think of these different attitudes as if they were a reflection of the 'seriousness' of the heroin problem in the two localities from which they originate, because Keith lives in an area where the heroin problem is indisputably more serious and extensive than where Linda and Brian live. Nor is experimentation with injection techniques completely unknown in Keith's locality, and there were some heroin addicts in his neighbourhood for whom injection was the preferred mode of administration. But there was no evidence to suggest that there was a drift among heroin users towards injection, and within the local drug culture among which he moved, 'chasing' was undoubtedly the dominant style of heroin use, as it had been when the drug first became available in the early 1980s. However, under such circumstances where injection techniques remain a largely unknown terrain within the local drug culture, if and when individuals were occasionally tempted to experiment with injection then there was probably a higher risk of overdose. And this is because, given that injection is a more efficient mode of administering the drug, a person who experiments with injecting on a one-off basis will not have established a tolerance against a properly estimated purity and quantity of the drug for injection purposes, and might well overestimate how much to inject. One of our informants, for example, reported that although when she was smoking heroin she needed 1 gramme per day to avoid withdrawal sickness, she found 1/4 of a gramme sufficient when she switched to injection. It is true that injecting heroin carries more health risks than smoking the drug, but where the local drug culture is knowledgeable and experienced about injection techniques then this provides its own safeguards against the possibility of overdose.

The patterns and styles of heroin use therefore suffer from wide local and regional variations across a number of dimensions. In a later section we shall describe some of the typical features of a heroin-using career, tracing how people are introduced to the drug and their subsequent experiences with it, both in terms of paths to addiction and possible exit-routes to abstinence. But while these typical heroin-using careers can offer some general guidelines for approaches to health education, the extreme diversity of the heroin problem, as we have described it so far, suggests that health education strategies will have to be closely tuned to local needs and circumstances if they are to prove effective.

4 PROFESSIONAL AND AGENCY RESPONSES

The diversity within the heroin problem in Britain today represents a real challenge to health education, which is further intensified by variations in the responses and understandings of different public agencies towards the problem, as well as by the immensely varying pattern of voluntary effort which has gathered together within the past two years and which continues to expand in some localities without any clear sense of direction. There are a variety of different conflicts of interest and approach between these different sectors which we shall highlight in due course, but potentially the sharpest set of conflicts (both real and potential) exists between those with a professional interest in drug problems as against those with a closer personal involvement such as parents' groups. Voluntary effort in the drugs field is, of course, to be welcomed. But it should also be recognised that voluntary movements, such as parents' groups and self-help groups, can represent a significant 'populist' challenge to the role of expertise in the drugs field. The ideology of many mutual aid groups is populist in the sense that, in one way or another, they insist that, 'You cannot properly understand heroin unless you have experienced the problem within your own family.' These same groups can be intensely hostile towards particular kinds of professional specialisms, including high-status doctors and psychiatrists. These hostilities typically centre on certain forms of treatment, such as methadone maintenance, which is sometimes seen by self-help groups as merely substituting one kind of drug problem for another. Parents' groups in our experience are also typically, although not always, hostile to forms of health education advice which depend upon 'harm-minimisation' strategies which these groups tend to define as 'soft' measures which condone drug-taking. There are also sometimes hostilities between self-help groups and the police, according to which the police do not take the heroin problem seriously enough and allegedly fail to act on information about dealing networks supplied to them by ex-users and their families. Our main focus will be on the responses of public agencies to the emerging heroin problem, but this tangled web of relationships and potential conflicts is the background against which our discussion takes place.

An Approach to Inter-Agency Relationships

One of the aims of our research was to study not only how heroin misuse was manifesting itself in different localities across the North of England, but also to examine at a local level how different agencies approached drug problems and in what ways these problems made a different impact on the routine workloads of different agencies. The major reason for this approach was to reach a better understanding of the obstacles which might lie in the way of attempts to fashion more effective modes of inter-agency liaison in the drugs field.

In conceptualising this research strategy we had drawn upon the experience of various initiatives in the field of crime prevention where a major preoccupation in recent years has been how to create an improved multi-agency approach, evidenced in work such as that of the NACRO Safe Neighbourhoods Unit (cf. Bright and Petterson, 1984; Home Office, 1982; 1984). One outcome of work of this type is that it shows how although different public agencies can easily agree at a highly generalised level that crime is a problem, when it comes down to the detailed practicalities of establishing localised crime-prevention initiatives, clear differences of approach and style can emerge between these agencies which belie the generalised consensus.

Another useful source for our approach is a study conducted some years ago into inter-organisational perspectives on alcohol-related problems, which was funded by the Social Science Research Council (cf. Friend *et al.*, 1981). This research had examined how different professional groupings (general practitioners, social workers, health visitors, hospital services, the police, etc.) tend to develop different understandings of alcohol-related problems. These different understandings, it was suggested, arose both as a consequence of how alcohol problems made themselves felt in the routine work of different professionals, and also as a result of the ways in which different theories as to the causes of alcohol abuse and its likely remedies had been generated within the different occupational cultures. (For research on occupational cultures and how different world-views are developed within them, cf. Hughes, 1958; Davis, 1968; Becker, 1970.)

If we summarise this research very sketchily, Friend and his colleagues first suggested that alcohol-related problems were associated with a variety of different kinds of events: driving a vehicle while over the legally-defined limit of alcohol consumption; accidents or injuries at work, at home or in the street; the incurring of debts; marital violence or stress, or the neglect of children; absenteeism or poor performance at work, perhaps leading to unemployment; mental or physical ill-health, including cirrhosis or brain damage; the commission of a crime or violent act; etc.

The research then went on to establish that alcohol-related problems tended to present themselves in very different ways to different agencies and professionals. Social workers typically met alcohol-related problems in the shape of child neglect, domestic difficulties and housing problems. The police estimated that at weekends or late at night approximately 90 per cent of their work was alcohol-related, in connection with public disturbances, household disturbances and road traffic offences. General practitioners, on the other hand, spent very little time with declared alcohol problems, and when they did it was associated with physical ailments and illnesses. In the hospital service, alcohol-related problems were found in the work of the accident and emergency unit. For health visitors, their statutory obligations to mothers and children under five years meant that they came into indirect contact with alcohol abuse through the problems caused by a husband's excessive drinking, or where a mother had resorted to mixing alcohol with anti-depressant drugs as an attempt to combat depression.

Alcohol therefore did not 'mean' the same thing to these different agencies, which had also developed their own 'theories' as to the origins of alcohol problems, while basing their actions on different assumptions as to what should be done in practical terms. And given these wide disparities, it seemed hardly surprising that these different agencies experienced considerable difficulties in trying to coordinate their work within an effective 'inter-agency' strategy.

We had hoped that it might be possible to replicate some aspects of this work in our own research, and to explore whether such a range of responses and understandings could be detected in relation to heroin misuse. However, this has proved to be much more difficult than we had anticipated. As we have already stated, the heroin problem is at the moment a very scattered and localised phenomenon, so that in many localities heroin misuse was not recognised by public agencies as a significant aspect of their routine work. Moreover, even in those areas where the heroin problem is more firmly rooted, we found that there was such an unfamiliarity with the problem, that many professionals were simply confused and frustrated — not only with the absence of any clear guidelines as to how they should try to respond to drug-related problems, but also with the shortage and inaccessibility of specialist resources. In those areas worst affected, some agencies had inaugurated in-service training programmes and were in the process of allocating staff to specialist roles or coordinating functions. However, it is far too early to see what such schemes might amount to, or to assess their outcome.

Nevertheless, it is possible to offer some broad indications of different agency responses, because clear patterns did emerge in terms of how heroin makes an impact (or does not) on the routine work of non-specialist agencies such as the probation service, social services departments, education departments and the youth service. We also made contact with health visitors and community psychiatric nurses in some localities, although our impressions are that there is much more variability in their role from one area to another, depending on systems of liaison with other agencies and the emphasis given to opiate problems within local hospital psychiatry. Police drug squads were also consulted in each area, and it was interesting to find that their views on the local heroin scene often differed widely from other agencies, and in particular from locally prevailing medical definitions. Finally, contact was made with a number of drugs liaison committees which have been recently established, as well as parents' groups and other forms of community support groups. Our discussion of these issues will be ordered first around the responses of non-specialist agencies, and then of specialist agencies such as the medical profession and the police.

Non-Specialist Agency Responses

Among the non-specialist agencies it was without question the Probation Service which had most contact with heroin users (or ex-users) in its day-to-day operations. These contacts rarely seemed to flow directly from drug offences *per se*, and it was more likely that people would be known to the service by virtue of other forms of crime which were not necessarily 'drug-related crime' in the sense of crimes committed in order to support a heroin habit. In one part of Manchester, for example, a probation officer who had been set the task of studying the heroin problem in his team's catchment area was surprised to discover that most of the locally notorious user-dealers thereabouts had been known to the Probation Service in one way or another for some years, mainly because of offences which preceded their involvement with heroin. But in other areas probation officers would have people on their caseloads whose offences (primarily shoplifting) more clearly formed part of their pattern of heroin misuse, in that thay had become involved in crime in order to support their habits. In one Merseyside neighbourhood a probation officer reported that he was now seeing young men in their late teens and early twenties, who had become addicted to heroin and resorted to shoplifting without any previous criminal record. They were often 'good lads', he said, 'who just would not have been seen in the criminal justice system at all twelve months ago'.

Probation officers are required to prepare social enquiry reports for the courts in order to assist in sentencing decisions, and it was most commonly in this context that a person's drug misuse would come to light. Less frequently, a probation officer might have clients under his or her supervision who used heroin, in which case the officer might be able to offer an important counselling function. But in whichever way, probation officers displayed more awareness and understanding of the heroin problem than other professional groups. Even so, in many areas the Probation Service reported that heroin made little or no impact on staff workloads.

In comparison with the Probation Service, it was a uniform pattern that Social Services Departments had much less contact with heroin users. Almost without exception, social workers rarely came across heroin use in the context of their extensive supervisory work with young offenders, which came as something of a surprise to us, although it does confirm the view that heroin use is rare among young adolescents. Where a Social Services Department would be most likely to have contact with a heroin user would be as an adjunct to child-care issues. Typically, this would be when the parent (or parents) of a child considered to be 'at risk' of harm or neglect was discovered to be using the drug.

However, these cases were so infrequent that they did not constitute an accumulated body of knowledge or working practices, even in areas where other sources indicated an extensive heroin problem. So that in one area of Merseyside where probation officers felt besieged by clients whose problems included heroin misuse, a senior social worker had to struggle quite hard to recollect a small handful of heroin-related cases that had figured on his office caseload within the past twelve months.

Social workers were also typically faced with a role confusion in those heroin-related problems that they did encounter. This arose because the focus for social services intervention in the family was the welfare of a child 'at risk', which meant that social workers were not very well placed to offer help to the person in the family who was actually using heroin. As one social worker from Manchester described this dilemma, the heroin-using parent might say, 'Don't take my child away, I'll promise to get myself together soon.' However, in the parent's timescale 'soon' might mean within the next twelve months or so, which although it was a short enough period in the addict's life, could have a crucial impact on the child's developmental needs. Of course, this tug-of-war for the social worker's attentions and sympathies is not unique to drug-related problems, and it makes itself felt most notoriously in non-accidental injury cases.

It is probably worth saying in this context that the fact that someone is a heroin user does not necessarily mean that they cannot also be an adequate parent. A North American study of women heroin addicts has suggested that mothers who are heroin users face substantially more difficulties in 'taking care of business' than men, although this did not mean that these difficulties could not be surmounted (cf. Rosenbaum, 1981). In our own research we encountered small numbers of heroin users who had childcare responsibilities, some of whom had failed to support their families (although this failure might have preceded their heroin use) whereas others had been successful in sustaining their family commitments, and took considerable pride in their achievement. The outcome is probably determined most by important factors such as a person's access to supportive relationships and a network of friends or kin who can assist in childcare responsibilities where necessary, although factors such as these are common to many people's abilities to sustain effective parental roles, and access to a variety of material and emotional resources determines outcomes across a range of issues in family life (cf. Brown and Harris, 1978; Graham, 1984).

Social workers, then, tend to have little contact with heroin users, and where they do their statutory obligations will invariably mean that they are not well placed to offer help and guidance to those heroin addicts whom they do encounter. It takes very little imagination to see that where a social worker has been instrumental in removing a heroin-using parent's children into public care, it will be unlikely that the parent will then be able to relate to the social worker as a source of personal help within a trusting relationship. The constraints upon the actions of Social Service Departments are shaped to a large degree by the current climate of widespread concern about child abuse cases, so that it takes even less imagination to envisage the headline in the popular press should a Social Service Department, knowing a parent to be using heroin, allow a child home on trial, and risk public infamy if the rehabilitation plan should go wrong.

Education departments, the schools and youth service have a self-evident role to play in effective health education on drug problems, but almost without exception education departments responded to our postal enquiry by saying that heroin use was not considered by them to be a problem in schools. There is some indication in parts of Merseyside of a small and possibly growing heroin experimentation among young people aged 15–16 years, but elsewhere our enquiries drew a blank, although it seems likely that more detailed, localised investigations might reveal scattered pockets of concern. But if we set speculation to one side, then uniformly the drug problems encountered with this younger age group concern alcohol and solvent abuse. In one area of Manchester, for example, where there was a well-established pattern of heroin misuse among people in their early twenties, a local residents' association informed us that among young adolescents the major problem was rowdy behaviour in the streets after drinking cider.

Contacts with health visitors were also established in some localities, although these were not followed through in many areas because it seemed an unpromising line of enquiry. In one area health visitors were involved in an intimate system of liaison with the Social Services Department around enquiries into suspected cases of child abuse, so that when drug problems were occasionally found the perceptions of health visitors mirrored those of social workers, which have already been described. In another locality some hostility was evident between social workers and health visitors who felt that the Social Services Department did not always act in the interests of the child, allowing children to remain in the care of heroin-using parents, although our enquiries with the social workers in the same locality did not confirm this impression. And in yet another locality, where our independent enquiries had established that there was an extensive heroin network, the health visitors were rather surprised that they should be consulted about something which was not their business. 'That doesn't concern me,' said one worker in this office. 'I'm a school nurse.'

Our impressions of the involvement of community psychiatric nurses were equally varied. In one district where plans for the development of a community-oriented drug programme were already well advanced, community psychiatric nurses were clearly key personnel with funds of local knowledge on patterns of drug misuse, and in all cases follow-up visits were attempted to the homes of people who had been through a detoxification programme. By comparison, in a different locality where a neighbouring hospital ran a 28-day methadone-reduction programme, none of the community psychiatric nurses who were interviewed had experience of following up patients who had been through detoxification. A variety of reasons were offered for this policy, including the feeling that drug users did not want any kind of follow-up because they usually discharged themselves and 'were only interested in getting back to their friends'. It was also stated that heroin addiction was not a nursing problem, because it was the person's own fault. This moralistic attitude was reflected in another district where a hospital-based social worker rarely arranged follow-up visits to people who had completed a methadone withdrawal programme. She confessed that she had become 'more cynical' through her contacts with drug addicts over the years, viewing them as people who did not really want to be helped, whereas she was less cynical about her dealings with alcoholics and not at all about psychiatric patients because they had a 'genuine illness'.

With varying degrees of emphasis, this general pattern of response was confirmed across the Northern region. Probation officers were those most likely to have contact with heroin users, although not usually as a direct consequence of drug misuse. Social workers were much less likely to have any contact, except as an adjunct to some form of child-care proceeding in a limited number of cases, and in some districts where our enquiries indicated the existence of a heroin network Social Services Departments reported confidently that from their experience there was no problem in the area. Education

22

departments and the youth service, including both the school psychological service and the schools themselves, were even less likely to report that heroin use was a problem for them. And in the case of health professionals such as health visitors and community psychiatric nurses we found a very varied response depending on local policy, although the scattered nature of our enquiries with these particular professional groups would make us more cautious in identifying any regular pattern.

Specialist Agencies: The Pro-Active Role

Having examined the responses of non-specialist public agencies to the heroin problem, we must now turn to those which include a specialist function: the medical profession and the police. And in doing so, it is important to bear in mind a vital difference between these two different professional groups, other than their specialist functions.

The agencies that have been considered so far have a largely reactive role in the drugs field, in that they are wholly dependent on external factors such as the availability of specialist resources and services of different kinds, as well as the size and shape of the local drugs problem. In the case of the medical profession and the police, however, there is a substantial difference in that they also have a pro-active role by which they can determine not only what specialist facilities will be made available, but through which their actions and policies can have important consequences in shaping some of the characteristics of the drug problems that are experienced in an area.

An obvious point is the prescribing policy of local medical practitioners (whether in specialist drug posts or not) which can measurably alter which drugs are available locally and in what quantities. For example, wherever there is a heroin problem then methadone has a street value. However, the indications of our research are that its price can double in an area where a methadone-maintenance policy has been discontinued by the local drug dependency unit or hospital clinic. Prescribing policy can sometimes have quite a dramatic impact upon not only the street value of methadone, but also on wider patterns of drug availability and drug choices. So that in one area where methadone and other substitutes had been more easily available for some years because of local prescribing policies, all our knowledgeable informants (including the drug squad and local drugs counselling agency) confirmed that maybe as much as 50 per cent of opiate misuse revolved around illicit pharmaceuticals, rather than imported street heroin. Moreover, since Diconal had become scarce, drug users in this locality had shown great persistence and ingenuity in finding substitutes for their preferred opiate, rather than switching to street heroin. These practices included crushing up a brand-name travel sickness pill, containing small quantities of dipipanone, together with Valium for injection purposes. In other areas where Diconal had been formerly widely used, there was evidence that the 'Diconal vacuum' was being filled by Palfium.

One further way in which local practices can influence drug choices and the health risks associated with these choices is the availability of syringes and needles through chemist shops and other outlets in those areas where injection is the preferred mode of heroin administration. In one town in the North-West where injection practices dominated the local scene, syringes and needles had been easily available through a particular retail pharmacy. However, when this shop recently closed down medical practitioners noted a sudden upsurge in the number of hepatitis cases in the town, which seemed to be directly attributable to the fact that the scarcity of syringes had led to an increase in the practice of sharing needles among heroin users. In response to this crisis a discreet health education campaign on 'harm-minimisation' lines had been launched through a local community newspaper, outlining the dangers of unhealthy injection practices, and those sources with good local knowledge believed that this had helped to contain the problem

23

and had contributed to an improvement of injection techniques within the heroin-using community.

Undoubtedly the most important way in which medical practices have a 'pro-active' influence depends upon whether methadone maintenance is available within an area, as opposed to where local policy had adopted an abstinence model whereby heroin substitutes are only available within the context of a phased withdrawal programme. It is outside the scope of our research to assess the relative merits or demerits of different approaches to the treatment and rehabilitation of heroin addicts, and it is not our intention here to enter into the debate on maintenance versus abstinence (cf. Trebach, 1982). Indeed, on the available evidence there would appear to be arguments on both sides, and perhaps the most appropriate policy option would be to allow some flexibility in locally available treatment resources. However, as things stand this is not the case. The field is characterised by sharp professional antagonisms between rival schools of thought, reflected in wide disparities in regional and local policies on this issue, making for a further element of diversity within the heroin problem and professional responses to it. This adds to the complexity of the health education task in relation to heroin misuse. Where one of the aims of health education is to offer guidance on available treatment facilities, and to direct drug users towards the most appropriate resources, then it follows that health education strategies will have to adapt themselves to these different circumstances if they are to be relevant to the needs and patterns of resource availability within any given locality. The educational and training needs of relevant non-specialist professionals will also differ for the same reasons.

We can offer some brief illustrations of how these different policies can make an impact on the local drugs situation, on the basis of interviews with heroin users and ex-users in areas which fell within the orbit of different treatment regimes. Where methadone maintenance is available, sometimes with a requirement that a person attends counselling sessions or group meetings, there can be no doubt that it can enable heroin users to bring some stability into their lives and hopefully act as a staging-post towards becoming eventually abstinent from opiates. The major benefit, as it was described to us, was that methadone maintenance released the heroin user from the need to 'hustle' in order to finance his or her habit — often by illegal means — and thereby to begin to rebuild some steadier rhythm in one's daily life and relationships.

By contrast, where the abstinence model is the only treatment option on offer, the heroin user is faced with a stark choice between continuing to use opiates or stopping completely. Those who support the abstinence model argue that this offers the heroin user a less complicated set of choices, thereby clarifying treatment goals by removing the constant bargaining process between clinic staff and users over how much methadone should be prescribed — a conflict vividly described by Stimson and Oppenheimer (1982) in their study of London clinics in the 1970s.

In one area of Manchester we had several meetings with a self-help group of heroin users who had embraced this abstinence ideology with good effect. Methadone, in their view, simply substituted one drug problem for another, whereas coming off heroin 'clean' without the use of methadone offered a clear goal to a heroin user who had discovered the motivation to do something about his or her drug misuse. By offering each other mutual support, both during withdrawal from heroin and in the ensuing months when 'staying off' heroin so often comes to be understood as a more difficult problem than 'coming off', they were helping to turn the tide within the peer-group of their neighbourhood against heroin use and steadily attracting new members to the self-help network.

A different response to the unavailability of methadone, from another area, was evidenced by the difficulties of a woman in her early thirties who had been financing her heroin habit by prostitution for some time. At one point she had entered a detoxification

24

programme when she found that withdrawal was not too difficult, but when she returned to her friendship network of heroin users she quickly relapsed. Now, some months on, she was growing tired of her lifestyle, but feared that she was unable to cope as things stood without the cushioning effect of opiates. What she would really like to do, she said, was to obtain a methadone-maintenance prescription which would enable her to bring some 'normality' back into her life, but this was simply not available where she lived. Without the necessary support, either personal or professional, to sustain anything like a commitment towards abstinence she had taken a decisive step in order to reduce the financial requirements of her habit and switched from smoking to injecting. So that whereas when she was 'chasing' she needed to smoke a gramme a day in order to 'keep straight', now she could get by on a quarter of a gramme.

These two contrasting experiences — the self-help group which shows a measure of success, and the relapsed addict who escalated her involvement with heroin towards injection—indicates how an abstinence model thrusts a heroin user who has become disillusioned with the habit back onto the resources of the local drug culture. Where these local influences are benign, as in the first case, leaders within a peer-group can help to turn local opinion against heroin involvement (cf. Hughes and Crawford, 1972). Where the supportive structures of friendship and guidance operate in a different direction, as in the second case, the outcome is quite opposed.

If the abstinence model might be thought of as a *'laissez-faire'* approach which leaves the fate of individuals to be fashioned by the prevailing circumstances within the local drug culture, the availability of methadone maintenance can radically alter an addict's perceptions of his or her problems — and not necessarily for the better. In one locality where methadone-maintenance was available, without any requirement to engage in counselling, we interviewed several heroin users who asserted that they were 'off drugs' even though they were taking hefty daily doses of oral methadone, some of them occasionally 'cranking up' with injectable methadone, which was available from the same medical source. Ex-users and their families in this area had come to accept a particular 'medical' definition of their difficulties, whereby heroin was described as a 'drug' and a problem, whereas methadone was seen as a 'medicine'. The availability of methadone had undoubtedly enabled a small circle of heroin users in this town to stabilise their lives to some extent, and some had eventually become abstinent. But for others this was rather a listless sort of accomplishment, and there was little evident motivation to become opiate-free other than a fitful lip-service to reducing their methadone dosage. In one family where a 20-year-old daughter had stopped using heroin and started taking prescribed methadone, there was an active confusion in the minds of family members as to the status of her drug involvement. On the one hand, she had reduced her contacts with the heroin subculture and she was no longer shoplifting in order to support her habit. But when she had first started taking methadone she had used it excessively, so that she would occasionally 'gouch out' on it. Her family had subsequently encouraged her to control her intake, although one suspected that this was an ongoing struggle, and she appeared to be making no real progress towards reducing her daily dosage by stages. Nevertheless, her brother tried to stress the positive side of his sister's condition, by using the term 'medicine' to legitimate her continuing dependence on opiates:

> 'She's got past stage of using heroin, hasn't she? And she's helping hersen now. And I don't take it as same, you know tekking medical stuff like linctus or owt like that. I don't think it's same as heroin.' (Wayne, 19 years, South Yorkshire)

The availability of methadone clearly had an ambiguous effect on this ex-user's family, and in the same locality we encountered similar confusions for other ex-users and their families. A peculiar form of hostility towards the local drugs counselling agency was also expressed by some ex-users in this area. This was partly because they suspected that the existence of the counselling service might constitute a threat to the continuation of their methadone prescriptions. But some people had also developed a belief that counselling and group therapy filled your head with 'all kinds of weird ideas'. As one man described it, methadone helped to sort out 'the physical side', but it did not 'help to straighten out your head, you have to do that yourself'. This man expressed no interest whatsoever in the local counselling service, while another in the same locality described the prescribing doctor — who did not offer any form of counselling as an adjunct to methadone maintenance —as 'the most liked person in the junkie society, because he's sympathetic'.

We can see, then, how variations in prescribing policies can lead to different sets of attitudes within the local drug culture, although it would be wrong to think of these attitudes simply being 'imposed' by different medical policies. Rather, it would seem that these different attitudes come about through subtle interactions between the local drug culture and prevailing medical beliefs. Nevertheless, the 'pro-active' power of the medical profession determines the overall context within which heroin users must come to terms with their drug misuse, and within which non-specialist agencies must work.

We can also indicate some of the ways in which the 'pro-active' role of the police, by adopting different strategies towards criminal investigation, can have a determining influence upon the way in which the heroin problem is experienced locally. In some areas the police have taken the view that a high priority must be given by the drug squad to sophisticated and time-consuming methods of surveillance which might enable the police to penetrate the upper reaches of the heroin economy. In this way it is hoped to bring effective prosecutions against people who are dealing in sizeable quantities of the drug, rather than to remain satisfied with arrests among the fraternity of small-scale user-dealers in the lower reaches of the street market, and it is easy to see how such a policy might seem attractive within the prevailing moral and political climate.

However, such a policy can have an adverse effect at a local level, in that surveillance operations must mean that small user-dealers are allowed to operate quite openly in some neighbourhoods over long periods of time, often to the alarm and annoyance of other local residents. It is a policy which can thus have the unfortunate consequence of leading to poor relationships between the police and the public, with local community groups questioning whether the police are taking the drugs problem in their locality seriously enough. It is also a policy which, by allowing user-dealers to operate with relative freedom, can increase the risks that heroin will begin to circulate within the neighbourhood peer-group. Because where heroin is available, there will always be peer-group leaders who will be tempted to experiment with the drug.

In other areas the police seem to be much less preoccupied with making major arrests of large-scale drug traffickers, so that they are quite prepared to take action against even small user-dealers at the 'messy' end of the heroin market. On the basis of a comparison between different areas it is our impression that where such a policy has been adopted it has encouraged the heroin-using population to remain inward-looking and reclusive, in sharp contrast to those neighbourhoods where there are highly visible user-dealer networks which are seen by local residents, quite understandably, as a threatening nuisance. These differences can also have a marked impact upon the morale of a neighbourhood, thus influencing the extent to which local groups of residents feel that they can take steps which might contribute locally towards the prevention of drug misuse. The ripple-effects of these problems can also reach far beyond the specific confines of drug abuse. In one locality with a highly visible heroin problem a general practitioner reported that the major impact of heroin misuse on his own workload was to be found among the elderly who often consulted him in a state of high anxiety, as a result of local heroin misuse and associated crime, and who sometimes felt unable to continue their independent life in the community because of these fears and were requesting admission to an old people's home.

26

The 'pro-active' role of the police, by which varying strategies of policing the heroin problem have been adopted in different areas, can have a broad impact upon the quality of life in a neighbourhood. It suggests a need for close consultation between the police and other relevant authorities and voluntary bodies in determining the police role. It might also indicate a significant tension between national priorities and local priorities in the policing of drug trafficking, which will no doubt be influenced by the recent establishment of a new drugs intelligence unit at national level.

Cooperation and Conflict in Drugs Liaison

We have described some of the diverse ways in which different public agencies are responding to the problem of heroin misuse in the northern towns and cities, and it is important to stress that these widely varying practical responses are by no means haphazard. Rather, they reflect the different ways in which drug problems make an impact upon their routine workloads, as well as differing philosophies which underpin their roles and tasks.

In the face of potential conflicts and misunderstandings such as those that we have already outlined, various drug liaison initiatives have been implemented with the aim of improving inter-agency cooperation and coordination. We were able to identify more than thirty initiatives of this kind across the North of England, indicating a growing awareness of the need for effective liaison between different interest groups. Nevertheless, enthusiasm for improved inter-agency liaison needs to be tempered with a recognition of some quite fundamental and inescapable divisions within the drugs field.

At the most general level there are three quite separate spheres of concern and practical action: (i) treatment and rehabilitation; (ii) education and prevention; and (iii) distribution and supply, that is, policing. Each of these different spheres of concern has its own basis of legitimation, and each is equally important in its own way. However, this does not mean that they are necessarily easy to reconcile with each other, and the potential for inter-organisational strain is considerable within any attempt to fashion a more effective system of inter-agency liaison.

For example, in those areas where methadone maintenance is available there is room for sharp conflicts of interest between the medical profession and the police, who are inclined to consider that the policy of prescribing methadone on an out-patient basis has the effect of creating an added dimension to the local street market for drugs. On the other hand, in one area where methadone is available on prescription this policy was justified to us partly on the grounds that it reduced the need for heroin users to engage in crime, and thus had the effect of reducing crime locally and thereby lessening the impact of the heroin problem on the wider community. (This is a position which has been argued most vigorously by Trebach, 1982.) However, police drug squads disagreed openly with such an argument when we put it to them. Nor is it a point of view that would find support with some of the parents' groups whom we consulted, where we heard loud complaints against medical practitioners who were prepared to prescribe methadone and other substitutes, on the grounds that such a prescribing policy was 'soft' on drug misuse. 'The junkie's friend' was the term used repeatedly to describe a prescribing doctor in one heated and emotional meeting of a parents' group that we attended.

If different treatment approaches can provoke controversy such as this, then so do different health education strategies. Health education can be roughly subdivided into two categories in the drugs field. On the one hand, there are policies which attempt to reduce the general level of demand for drugs, thus going for outright prevention. But there are also policies which assume that drug use cannot be completely eliminated and which under the title of 'harm-minimisation' or 'risk-minimisation', offer to people who persist in using drugs such advice as might minimise the harm which they do to themselves. In the case of heroin, for example, the health hazards associated with smoking are in all probability less than those associated with injecting. Or, where heroin users persist in injecting, there are elementary health precautions which can be taken: such as using clean syringes and sterilised water, not sharing needles with other users, etc. In our subsequent discussion we refer to these two different styles of health education as 'preventive' and 'harm-minimisation' strategies.

Whatever the relative merits of these different approaches, once again we encountered sharp division of opinion between different interest groups, with the most clear division existing between professional and non-professionals. 'Harm-minimisation' strategies seemed capable of provoking most controversy. Broadly speaking, we found that professionals recognised that these could make an important contribution to drugs education. Even so, there was sometimes a reluctance to become publicly associated with 'harm-minimisation' strategies because of the hostility which can be directed against them. This hostility was particularly evident among some parents' groups who, once again, see this as a 'soft' option which condones drug use. This was not always the case, although parents' groups did tend to favour a policy directed towards outright 'prevention'.

The recent government-sponsored advertising campaign, with its slogans 'Heroin Screws You Up' and 'How Low Can You Get on Heroin?', is undoubtedly intended as a 'preventive' strategy. Among different groups of professionals we encountered very few people who were openly enthusiastic about this campaign. The vast majority were coolly neutral, while a significant minority regarded the campaign as ill-conceived and more likely to glamorise heroin than to deter potential users. The Drug Indicator Project research in North London offers some support for the view that by stressing the dangers involved in heroin use, this offers a 'macho' challenge to some young men that they can 'handle it' and so prove their manhood through a mortal contest with the demon drug (cf. O'Bryan, 1985). Research in New York in the 1960s also showed how the notoriety of heroin could provide the opportunities by which young men could establish a 'stand-up cat' status within their peer-group (cf. Feldman, 1968; Fiddle, 1976).

We found some support for such a view in our research. In one area of Merseyside, for example, a social worker with extensive experience with young offenders expressed some surprise that it tended to be the most intelligent and adventurous young people who were likely to experiment with heroin, and not as one might expect those who were gullible and easily led. Young people who were slower-witted, or who might even have been classified as educationally subnormal, were in his experience genuinely afraid of heroin and unwilling to accept the challenge. Whereas those with a local reputation to defend as 'Jack the Lad', who had proved in the past that they could face and outfront challenges to their developing manhood, were the leaders in experimentation with drugs as in most things. Among an older age group in a Manchester suburb, it was again said to be peer-group leaders who were the first to try heroin when it became available. And in Humberside an experienced youth worker thought that if heroin were more freely available, then he knew some young people who would be likely to experiment: 'One or two think heroin is dangerous and it would be exciting to try it, and particularly if "Maggie" is telling them it's no good then it must be worth having a go.'

Among heroin users and ex-users we found a variety of responses to the advertising campaign. There was perhaps an inevitable tendency for some people to be cynical about the campaign, although it was often acknowledged that it was probably not directed at people like themselves who already had a well-established pattern of drug misuse. One important criticism which came through in a variety of ways was that the campaign was likely to be counter-productive because of the way in which it stressed the enslavement produced by heroin and the horrors of withdrawal, which might deter some people who were using heroin from trying to come off it by their own efforts. But other people thought that the campaign did not go nearly far enough, and that if it was intended to frighten children and young people then it should be more blood-curdling. One young woman in Liverpool thought that the small posters in cafés which warned that your friendships would be damaged were a true description, but that the television advertisements and hoardings were an exaggeration; and she wondered whether the people whom they depicted were 'proper heroin addicts' or actors. When informed that they were probably actors, she said: 'Hm, I thought so. I can tell a smack head anywhere, and no one's that far gone.'

One obvious difficulty with the government advertising campaign, reflected in the widely varied responses to it that we collected, is its failure to identify clearly its specific target audiences. What might frighten a boy or girl of 14 years can prove wickedly funny to hardened heroin users in their late-twenties. But a much more serious difficulty, testified to by the experiences of many of the heroin users whom we met, is that they often first experimented with heroin even after they had seen the damaging effect which it had produced in the lives of their friends. These were people who did not need television advertisements to warn them of 'How low can you get on heroin'; they had experienced it at close quarters, and yet this knowledge did not deter them from eventually trying the drug and becoming addicted themselves:

> 'It had been there for years before I tried it. I remember two years before I ever got into it a mate of mine was having it, and he'd offer it me then. I was scared like, "No way, I'm not touching that" like. But two years later that's when I started, gradually sort of come round . . . It was weird. I always said, everyone says, "I won't get hooked on it", and you never think it will . . . you never think it will happen to you. I was having it every day, and I was thinking to myself, "Oh, I'll have to be careful with this". 'Cos when I first started having it most of my mates were addicts then, like, so I knew what it could do to people. I thought, "I'd better be careful with this" . . . So I'd had it every day, a bit every day . . . this was just a bag with two mates, and I'd say to myself, "I'd better just not have none and see what happens", to see if I'd start turkeying. And I'd leave it for a full day, and I'd feel OK and I'd think, "Oh I must be all right then, I'm not turkeying". So I'd go and have it the next day. And it'd go on like that for weeks. Until, finally, I left it for two days and on the second day I just started, really bad, turkeying like . . . I thought, "Shit".'
> (Jack, 22 years, Merseyside)

Jack's sorry tale touches very directly on the conflict between 'preventive' and 'harm-minimisation' strategies. The 'preventive' education of his friends' experiences had not deterred him, although he understood the need to be cautious and he had tried to take elementary precautions against the possibility of becoming addicted by occasionally abstaining. But his precautions were deeply flawed. What Jack clearly did not know is that where patterns of non-addictive heroin use on a recreational basis have been identified, principally within the 'chipping' culture of North America, stable non-addictive opiate use is only sustained when people adhere to strict rules about the frequency of use (cf. Zinberg, 1984). And one of these rules is that the drug is only taken *very* occasionally, and never on consecutive days. If heroin is used on a daily basis over a period of weeks, as Jack used it, then addiction will follow as sure as night follows day. It is of course impossible to know whether Jack would have been able to avoid addiction, if he had been supplied with effective 'harm-minimisation' advice. But without it, he stood absolutely no chance whatsoever.

The potential conflicts that we have identified so far concern matters which divide opinion in response to specific strategies of health education and different treatment philosophies. A further set of conflicts are brought into play when we turn to drug liaison initiatives which attempt to cut across the boundaries between treatment, health education and policing. These are particularly evident in the common problems faced by various mutual aid groups such as parents' groups and community support groups which, along with drug liaison committees, are proliferating in some parts of the North —but in such a way that without established guidelines they are quite literally having to 'make it up as they go along'.

One area of difficulty repeatedly experienced by these voluntary initiatives at some stage in their development is the question of their involvement with the police. In most instances these groups were established in order to offer help and support to drug users and their families, and sometimes where there is more formal involvement by statutory agencies to establish centres for advice and counselling. Police involvement poses a difficult choice for these groups because it is feared that if they are seen to be too closely involved with law enforcement agencies, then they might risk losing the trust of drug users and their families who are their target population. In one instance the question of whether a probation officer should be admitted to membership of a liaison committee was also scrutinised very carefully, because of the close association between the Probation Service and the courts. And in another instance the local police, having been instrumental in establishing a drug liaison committee, then withdrew because they felt that their participation might prejudice the aims of the committee to offer support and counselling on a confidential basis to drug users and their families.

The role of the police in health education programmes is another area of great interest and potential conflict, with evidence of wide variations in existing practices. In some areas drug squads seem happy to accept invitations to visit schools and youth clubs in order to give talks on drug questions, in a similar way that the police have traditionally offered advice on road safety. However, in one of these areas a major youth centre had discontinued this practice because it was felt that the police suffered a role-conflict, in that visiting officers seemed far too curious about the drug-using habits of youngsters attending the club, which was hardly calculated to encourage trust and an open discussion of drug choices.

In other areas the police seem less sure that drugs education is their proper function, and in one district a policy had been adopted only to give demonstrations and educational talks to groups of people over 18 years of age. Here we were informed that the police were in agreement with the report of the Advisory Council on the Misuse of Drugs on Prevention (ACMD, 1984) that drugs education should be integrated within a general health curriculum in schools, and that to single out drug questions for special mention risked glamorising the issue. The role of the police in health education, whether through drug squads or community liaison functions, is a matter which deserves further scrutiny.

If these examples illustrate a cautious approach towards police involvement in community initiatives, there were also instances where parents' groups and community groups took a different stance. In these cases the group did not define itself as a support group, but had moved towards a 'pressure group' function in order to campaign for increased resources, including more effective policing. Under these circumstances parent and community groups encouraged police involvement and were happy to supply information to the police on the whereabouts of local dealing networks. Moreover, in some meetings that we attended these groups were also prepared to discuss (if not actually implement) vigilante-style direct action against local dealers. It is of course the highly publicised direct action tactics of some community groups, especially those in Dublin as described by McCann (1984), which inclines some parent and community groups to be wary of police involvement. Because of this publicity, which has tended to de-emphasise the other useful functions which these groups can serve, heroin users will readily assume that parents' groups have only one purpose in mind, which is to inform on local drug networks. In such circumstances the only way that a local group can sometimes convince its target audience that it does not aim to 'grass them up' is to distance themselves overtly from the police, although this does not mean that they are hostile to the police. On the contrary, if anything it is those groups who have moved towards 'pressure group' tactics who are more likely to be critical of the police, whom they see as providing an inadequate service.

The role of the police will necessarily loom large in the formation of liaison committees and other community initiatives because of the illegal nature of the heroin trade, and it is our impression that parents' groups and community groups will inevitably face this difficult choice about police involvement at some stage in their development. There is even a real possibility that some initiatives of this kind might founder on this conflict, and on several occasions we have noted groups where an uneasy tension existed between group members who disagreed on what their proper role should be. In one instance a founder-member of a successful parents' group which had been in existence for some time told us privately that she was thinking of leaving the group because the 'hang 'em and flog 'em brigade' were becoming too vocal, which threatened to jeopardise the original aim of the group which was to sponsor mutual aid between the parents of drug users. Here as elsewhere, what this experience indicated was that the centrality which the role of the police assumed in these disputes was largely of a symbolic nature: one which focussed a live tension as to whether community initiatives and liaison committees were concerned with 'care' or 'control'.

Another active source of tension in drug liaison initiatives arises from the fact that they often have a multi-drug focus. This need not be a problem if participants are willing to share and learn from each other. But we have already indicated that different public agencies hold widely varying views as to the most worrying form of drug misuse, which can mean that large parts of a drug liaison committee's agenda will seem 'irrelevant' to many participants for much of the time. Education departments, for example, are most likely to focus on solvent abuse as a serious problem among children of school age — but it is in the nature of solvent abuse that it visits schools and neighbourhoods in epidemic fits-and-starts, so that at any one time it can either be seen as an all-consuming No. 1 problem, or completely absent from the local agenda. Social services departments, on the other hand, tend to view alcohol abuse as their most pressing problem, especially through its association with domestic violence, and alcohol-related problems are endemic to our society. Whereas drug counselling agencies in some areas report that problems with medically prescribed tranquillisers constitute a growing proportion of self-referrals to them, possibly stimulated by the BBC 'That's Life' survey of tranquilliser problems (Lacey and Woodward, 1985).

All this will tend to mean that some interest groups will become impatient when 'their' problem is not the centre of attention in a drugs liaison committee's business. Drug squad officers, for example, have confided to us that they view it as a waste of valuable time to sit around discussing problems with legal drugs such as alcohol and tranquillisers. And in the case of mutual-aid groups, we have encountered situations where the parents of opiate users were scandalised by the suggestion that tobacco and alcohol were much more significant health problems in the community as a whole than heroin. This simply confirmed their view that it was only possible to understand drug problems from first-hand experience within one's own family.

As far as heroin misuse is concerned, we have already indicated that it tends to have only a peripheral importance for non-specialist public agencies, so that it would be unrealistic to expect them to place a high priority on the involvement of their personnel in any kind of liaison initiatives directed against heroin abuse. Indeed, even those specialist agencies with day-to-day contact with the heroin problem do not necessarily see eye-to-eye about the nature and scale of the problem. It came as something of a surprise to us, for example, to discover that the police in some areas were quite sceptical about the scale of heroin use in their district, in some instances finding themselves in sharp disagreement with statistical estimates that had been produced from medical sources, including those contained in the DHSS survey, *Drug Misuse, Prevalence and Service Provision* (DHSS, 1985). In the police view, especially in some areas to the east of the Pennines, the size of the heroin problem had been vastly inflated in those estimates.

Finally, in this discussion of potential conflicts within drugs liaison initiatives we turn to the role of parents' groups and similar voluntary initiatives. These have emerged within the past few years both at a national and local level in a number of guises and under a variety of different titles: Parents Against Drug Abuse; Families Anonymous; Parents in Pain; Action Against Drug Abuse; Parents' Helpline; Families Against Drug Abuse; Narcotics Anonymous; Drug Users Advice Line; Drugs Support Group; etc. Sharing neither common origins, nor a common philosophy, some were established with professional assistance or even at the instigation of professional agencies, whereas others are truly 'grass roots' developments. Whatever their origins, the driving force behind them tends to be the parents of drug-users and ex-users, and they embrace a variety of ideologies: from those who recommend that one's drug-using offspring should be 'loved' and 'cherished' whatever problems they inflict upon the family, to those who urge a more confrontational stance, or those like the national organisation Families Anonymous which advises families to allow addicts to hit rock-bottom so that they are forced to seek help for themselves. In one recent commentary on the heroin problem it is suggested that family groups tend to be largely middle-class in orientation (cf. Picardie and Wade, 1985) although this does not reflect our experience in the North of England where working-class families are commonly members of these groups, and they differ among themselves in a number of other ways. Sometimes they will include a counselling function, especially where there had been professional involvement, although it seems to be more common that they act as self-help and mutual-aid groups. Indeed, parents' groups are sometimes suspicious of counselling services offered by professionals. As a founder-member of one parents' group in North-East Lancashire explained: 'Unless you've taken drugs or lived as a parent with drug-takers, then our view is that you can't begin to understand what it's all about.'

This essentially 'populist' stance of some parents' groups can make for uneasy tensions between such voluntary initiatives and the services that are offered by public agencies and professionals. We have already described how parents' groups can be quite hostile towards prescribing doctors, methadone-maintenence programmes, or 'harm-mini-misation' health education strategies which they define as being 'soft' on drugs. But there is also evidence of a suspicious attitude among professionals towards some of the practices embraced by voluntary groups. According to an experienced student counsellor attached to a further education college in a Lancashire town, parents' groups in his experience tended to become 'permanent confessionals' which did not help many people and which easily ran out of steam. Indeed, in several places we learned of parents' groups which had disbanded once the initial enthusiasm had dissipated. A drugs agency worker in another area who had been involved in helping to set up a number of self-help groups said that once they were established he tended to leave them to manage their own affairs, even though this might mean that they became directionless: 'It gets boring sitting around listening to people moaning all day, a million and one personal heartaches . . . it may help some people, but not everyone. They're best left to themselves anyway, because they don't like being told what to do.'

What these professional discontents allude to are the practices that have been adopted by some parents' groups whereby entire sessions are devoted to what was known in one group as 'sharing', a routine in which all participants were required to take it in turns to offer personal testimony to their difficulties and to 'share' their experiences with drug problems. As a means of ventilating their pent-up feelings in an accepting atmosphere,

32

this can undoubtedly offer relief to people in distress. However, it was a common professional view that there was too little structure in sessions such as these, and this only led to an unhelpful and unceasing out-pouring of feeling — a 'permanent confessional' in fact. In one area, within close geographical proximity, there was both a self-help parents' group and a family group run by a probation officer on more structured therapeutic lines. Some parents attended both sets of meetings, but expressed dissatisfaction with the 'family therapy' group and felt that their own 'sharing' sessions were better. In the probation officer's group, they said, he kept interrupting the flow and bringing them back to a preconceived focus. In the probation officer's view, on the other hand, unstructured 'sharing' sessions were probably only of limited short-term benefit, whereas his aim was to assist group members to gain an improved understanding of their difficulties and to structure their experience along therapeutic lines. He did nevertheless concede that the two forms of group experience might offer complementary benefits.

One problem at issue in these conflicts is the question of where responsibility lies for drug problems. A primary consideration within a counselling philosophy will be to encourage people to take responsibility for their own actions and problems. But in some parents' groups that we have met our impression was that they were often anxious to place the blame for their children's heroin use somewhere else. What one might describe as a 'demonology' is thereby constructed within some of these groups, according to which the heroin user is seen as the hapless victim of a range of alien forces: pushers, prescribing doctors, the influence of bad company, etc. A similar demonology has been noted in a study of parents' associations which are focused on the recruitment of young people into new religious movements such as the 'Moonies' (cf. Beckford, 1985).

But there is also evidence of good working practices in many parents' groups, and the 'confessional' itself can play an important role by showing new members that they are not alone in their difficulties and that it is possible to live with and express powerful emotions without buckling under the strain. The difficulty, as ever with 'grass roots' initiatives of different kinds, is sometimes how to reconcile their wilder enthusiasms with what can be offered by public agencies and professionals. Even so, the bitter criticisms which parents' groups sometimes advance against professional services reflect not only the intolerable anxieties and strained loyalties which the families of drug users often encounter, but also the real weaknesses and shortages of effective public provision.

In summary, there can be little doubt that improved liaison and coordination in the drugs field, together with closer links between statutory agencies and voluntary initiatives, would be a welcome development. However, what our research has shown in this area is that little purpose will be served by exhortations to 'cooperate' and 'coordinate', unless there is sufficient acknowledgement of legitimate areas of disagreement between different agencies which reflect their different tasks and responsibilities, together with other areas of mutual misunderstanding which are a common feature of inter-organisational relationships in most spheres of practical action. It would be wrong, in the light of the evidence gathered together, to assume that any single agency or interest group has the 'correct' view of the problem which must then be imposed upon other agencies and accepted by them. Differences in power between different public agencies is another characteristically difficult area in inter-organisational relations. One reason for the caution often shown towards police involvement in drug liaison initiatives would seem to be the fear that police preoccupations will come to dominate their work, simply because of the power of the police as a social institution. Voluntary bodies will sometimes be suspicious of statutory agencies for the same reasons, where powerful clinic-based medical specialisms are perhaps most frequently experienced as aloof and unresponsive to locally-felt needs.

For these kinds of reason it is equally important to recognise not only the promise of improved inter-agency liaison, but also its limits. The diversity of the heroin problem is such that it also requires a diverse repertoire of responses. The aims of drug liaison initiatives should be to sustain sufficient commitment between different interest groups that this allows for both cooperation and conflict. The challenge for health education — both with respect to heroin users and potential users, and also the educational needs of different professional interest groups and voluntary bodies — is how to target health education successfully to different audiences, and how to embrace the many-sided conflicts within this field of interest so as to enhance inter-professional and inter-agency understanding without belittling what are often quite rational sets of arguments and antagonisms.

5   BECOMING A HEROIN USER AND HEROIN-USING CAREERS

Finally, we must turn to a consideration of heroin users themselves. Why do people use heroin, and how are they first introduced to it? Can people control heroin use, so that it remains merely an occasional recreational pastime, or is addiction an inevitable outcome of experimentation? Why do people take such risks with their health when the dangers of heroin are so widely known, or are many people still ignorant of its addictive properties? Is the drug in fact enslaving as popular stereotypes insist, and are the horrors of withdrawal so engulfing as in the common notion of 'cold turkey'? Why is it that so many ex-addicts seem to say that 'coming off' is easy, but that 'staying off' is the most difficult part of abstinence?

Different Statuses of Involvement with Heroin

There is no such thing as a 'typical' heroin user, nor a typical heroin user's career. Nevertheless, it is useful to think in terms of a simple four-phase model to describe the different levels of involvement with the drug through which a heroin user's career will pass.

1. The non-user
2. The initial offer and experimentation
3a. Occasional use on a recreational basis
3b. The 'grey area' of transitional use
4. Addictive use

The non-user having been offered the drug, will either accept it or reject the offer. If the offer is accepted and the person tries it on an 'experimental' basis, they might either discontinue their experimentation quite quickly because they do not enjoy the experience, or they might embark on a more prolonged period of experimentation. At this point they might begin a pattern of recreational use on a very occasional basis, and continue this pattern over a long period of time without becoming addicted. Or they might begin to use the drug more frequently and enter upon what we have called the 'grey area' or transitional use where it is not clear, either to themselves or others, whether or not they are becoming addicted — a phase of heroin use open to widespread misinterpretation in terms of the person's status of involvement with the drug, which is why we choose to call it the 'grey area'. And finally, if this pattern of transitional use continues for any length of time, the heroin user will suffer an imperceptible drift into addiction.

Each of these phases can be thought of as different *statuses* of heroin involvement, and the passage between these different statuses as *transition points*. For health education purposes, these different statuses imply different *audiences,* with differing educational and informational needs. The transition points will also be crucial target areas for health education. Finally, each status will imply different possible *exit-routes* towards abstinence.

In moving from one status to another, conscious choices will sometimes make themselves apparent to the individual. But equally, a person can move imperceptibly from one status to another without any conscious decision-making. This is especially the case in the patterns of transitional use which take a person from the status of occasional user to compulsive user and addiction. At this fateful transition point it is not uncommon for heroin addicts to say that they were taken by surprise when they first experienced withdrawal symptoms, sometimes to the extent that they did not identify what these symptoms were.

There is nothing inevitable about the passage from one status to another in the career of a heroin user. Some people do slide rapidly into habitual use and addiction, following the pattern of progressive decline and escalating drug consumption which characterises the dominant stereotypical image of the heroin addict. But other people can, and do, arrest their involvement at different points in this hierarchy of statuses, so that some people discontinue their heroin use after a brief flirtation with the drug, whereas others maintain stable patterns of occasional use over a long period of time (cf. Zinberg, 1984). But because the hidden figure of experimental or recreational use is unknown, it is not possible to say what proportion of heroin users follow the pattern of progressive decline into addiction which is commonly (but wrongly) assumed to be the inevitable consequence of heroin use.

Exit-routes also vary considerably. Different motivations trigger them, different methods are used in order to come off heroin, and different timescales are involved. Some people try to make a clean break with heroin, while others try to withdraw themselves slowly by gradually reducing their intake. Some try to do it with professional assistance, whereas others do it on their own. And a crucial distinction must be made between 'coming off', which for many heroin users is relatively effortless, and 'staying off' which has been repeatedly described to us as much more difficult.

This simple model could undoubtedly be refined, and it will be overlaid with important considerations such as whether a person smokes heroin or injects it. For example, an exit-route for someone who injects might first involve moving on to smoking heroin for a time and overcoming 'needle fixation' before attempting to come off the drug completely. Nevertheless, this simple model will serve usefully as a framework for our subsequent discussion which will focus on crucial points of transition: the circumstances of the initial offer; experimentation and the perceived benefits of heroin use at this stage; the 'grey area' of transitional use into addiction; and finally exit-route and the process of 'coming off' and 'staying off' heroin.

However, first it is important to recognise that even habitual heroin use is compatible with a wide range of lifestyles and patterns of use (cf. Stimson, 1973; Stimson and Oppenheimer, 1982). And before moving on to a consideration of different statuses of involvement, it will be useful to exemplify what these different patterns of habitual use amount to, on the basis of experiences that we have gathered together in our research.

> Kevin started smoking heroin four years ago in a circle of friends. At its peak his habit amounted to 1 gramme of heroin daily. He supported his habit by shoplifting, for which he was caught more than once. It was when he was facing a further court appearance, which seemed likely to result in a custodial sentence, that he discovered the motivation to enter a treatment programme.

36

Joe had a pattern of heroin use, stretching back for nearly ten years, which involved episodic binges during which he would consume the drug hungrily. When he felt that his habit was spiralling out of control, he would register for a methadone-reduction programme whereupon he would remain abstinent for as long as 18 months before starting his next binge.

Julie maintained her heroin habit, and that of her boyfriend, for nearly two years by prostitution. At one time they were consuming 1½ grammes daily, costing something like £600 per week, which she said she could earn easily by a couple of hours work per night.

Linda and Brian struggled on for nearly three years injecting heroin which they purchased when their fortnightly social security giro came through. They were consuming no more than a gramme each fortnight, and when their supply ran out they would periodically go through withdrawal. Linda is now abstinent and Brian receives a methadone prescription.

Wendy had a boyfriend who used to offer her heroin occasionally which she at first refused although she eventually used it on a daily basis for six months. She quit at that time when she became afraid that she would be caught shoplifting which she realised would become an increasing necessity if she were to continue to use heroin. Even so, she said that she was 'never that much bothered' about heroin anyway, and did not find it too difficult to give up the drug.

Mick smoked heroin for two years and was spending £150 per week on his habit. On reflection he cannot really understand where the money came from. He never got into stealing or dealing in drugs, and borrowed most of his money from family and friends.

When Harry first tried heroin he had several thousand pounds in the bank, consisting largely of redundancy money from when he had been made unemployed. He quickly developed a heavy habit of more than a gramme smoked daily and was always generous with his friends who also smoked heroin, so that he blew all his money in a matter of months. When his debts began to increase he stopped using heroin and he now receives methadone.

Carol first tried heroin with a girlfriend, and says that she did not know what it was at the time. She became heavily involved with a circle of heroin users for 12 months, but she now received methadone while still buying a £5 bag of heroin every other week and enjoying 'a little toot'.

When asked about his drug involvements, Ronnie said that he did not know anything about heroin, only 'speed', 'barbs' and 'skag'. When then asked what 'skag' was, he said, 'Well it's a very dilute form of heroin I suppose'. He lived in an area where heroin was almost completely unknown, and seemed to think that there was a distinction between 'white' and 'brown' heroin, the latter seen as less powerful or dangerous. In any case, he said that he had only tried 'skag' once, by 'chasing the dragon', and it made him sick. He was not interested in trying it again.

The Initial Offer and Experimentation

Very little is known in any detailed way about early patterns of heroin use. The beginning user is elusive, and not only because the practice is illegal and therefore kept well hidden. A person who tries heroin will sometimes quickly discontinue use, either because they find that they are unable to maintain a supply of the drug, or because it makes them feel ill and they have no desire to continue. There is no reason why people such as this should come to the notice of public authorities or researchers. Only those who sustain their heroin use over time are likely to come to public notice, and then because of their involvement in crime, ill-health or domestic difficulties. There is no reason to suppose that the early experiences of those people who do come to public notice should correspond to the experiences of those who do not. So that what follows might only be a partial reconstruction of early experiences with heroin.

Nevertheless, a number of features of the circumstances of the initial offer can be briefly summarised.

1. The initial offer will always be made in the context of a friendship network.
2. The stereotype of the 'pusher' and the 'free sample', so beloved of the news media, is false and unhelpful for health education purposes.
3. There is no guarantee whatsoever that the known dangers of heroin will deter people from accepting the initial offer. Indeed, an emphasis on the dangers of heroin might sometimes even enhance the sense of risk and excitement to be enjoyed from the drug, and increase the likelihood that the initial offer will be accepted.
4. Nor is there any guarantee that because a person has refused an offer of heroin in the past, they will not accept in the future.

The first time that a person is introduced to heroin it will be by a friend, and not by a so-called 'pusher'. This point is so important that it cannot be emphasised too strongly. Indeed, this makes it more likely that the offer will be accepted, because the context of friendship (or kinship) will make the drug seem that much safer than if it had been offered by a stranger. It is indeed a sobering fact that if the sterotype of the 'pusher' and the 'free sample' to lure people into addiction were true, then its possibilities for epidemic growth within a friendship network would be considerably reduced.

When asked how they first got into heroin, our informants offered different versions of the same story:

'I was just gave some, for nothing like, by a mate. And the feeling is different, I liked the feeling... and after that I started buying my own bags, £5 bags and that, I just got into it that way.' (Colin, 23 years, Manchester)

'It's like everything else, the heroin came round and... I was curious so I tried it and I liked it.... There was a few of us, we were all good mates and that like, we all tried it and eventually everyone just got hooked.' (Eddie, 21 years, Merseyside)

It is not clear from these two accounts whether Colin and Eddie accepted heroin on the very first occasion that it was offered to them. But other people remembered quite clearly that at first they had been reluctant to get involved:

'My boyfriend's friends were all using it and that, and giving it to me .... They were always offering me chases, and at first I was refusing it, but then I gradually slipped into it.' (Josephine, 28 years, Humberside)

'How did you get into it yourself then?'

'Just through my mates really, going to their houses, and well one of my mates, he'd say, "D'you want a chase?" or whatever, and I just started getting into it like that... But it had been there for years before I tried it... a mate of mine was having it, and he'd offer it me then. I was scared like, "No way, I'm not touching that", like. But two years later that's when I started... and the next minute it was everywhere, like. It just sort of took Liverpool by storm.' (Jack, 22 years, Merseyside)

38

The Early Experience: Ethiopia or Utopia?

What does it feel like when a person first tries heroin? Often enough it makes them feel sick, and sometimes this is the end of their heroin-using career. But other people persist with heroin, in spite of the nausea, which is hardly surprising in view of the fact that initial encounters with other drugs (including those that are socially sanctioned, alcohol and tobacco) often make people feel ill until they learn how to take the drug properly and how to handle its effects and interpret them as enjoyable. The first surreptitious 'drag' or 'swallow' on a cigarette, with its attendant effects of dizziness or nausea; the 'never again' feeling which accompanies the first hangover, or the sickness from excessive drinking: these experiences lay a sound foundation upon which people will persist with drugs which are not immediately experienced as pleasurable, having learned that these are inhibitions which must be overcome if an intoxicant is to be enjoyed. And in this respect there is no reason why heroin should be different from other drugs.

If the likelihood that heroin will make someone feel ill cannot be relied upon to deter them from continuing use, then what are the pleasurable effects? Often in the accounts of ex-addicts we hear only of the painful and enslaving absorption into the drug; 'the monkey on your back'. But a major reason that people use, and continue to use heroin, is that they enjoy it. This is sometimes a difficult thing for health education to admit to, but it is true nevertheless.

Precisely what is the nature of this enjoyment? Here we enter into an area of difficulty, because drug users do not employ a very complex vocabulary by which to describe and label the internal states experienced when under the influence of a drug. So that words such as 'stoned', 'buzz', 'high' and 'wrecked' not only sum up the limits of this restricted vocabulary, but are also employed to describe the effects of a variety of substances (cannabis, amphetamines, opiates) which are otherwise totally dissimilar.

A typical description of the initial effects of heroin, then, will often be set in a characteristic vagueness:

> 'First, when I was on it, like, I dunno ... it made me feel dead pleasant, I dunno ... as if I never had a care in the world, d'you know what I mean? It wasn't like a "high" ... It was just like ... you haven't got a care, y'know, it was just different.' (Paul, 24 years, Merseyside)

Sometimes heroin's effects were described, in straightforward and immediate terms, as simply pleasurable:

> 'It was just the nicest drug going. You feel just great! Just ... phoo ... blows your mind, like, you start nodding and ...' (Eddie, 21 years, Merseyside)

> 'I thought it was the best, like, that I'd ever tried ... Sorry I did like (laughs) It was just, I don't know, different completely, just better.' (Joey, 20 years, Merseyside)

Some people described heroin's effects as peaceful and relaxing:

> 'With smoking, it comes on you gradually and you just feel dead relaxed and dead tired, and what have you ...' (Mick, 23 years, Manchester)

Whereas other people described the initial effects as a feeling of great personal power with an immediate impact:

> 'As soon as you chase it, it just hits you straightaway and you just feel like the boss, like ...' (Jack, 22 years, Merseyside)

And there were those who liked the helpless feeling of being 'wrecked' and 'gouching', which is a common British expression for the North American term 'nodding off', and which comes through in this Liverpudlian's version of drug argot as 'grouching':

> '*So what's so special about heroin?*'

> 'The way you take it. I loved it, like . . . . And the hit's brilliant . . . . You just sit there and just . . . like helpless. You must look bad and all that, because I've seen me mates and thought they did, like. And, I'm just sitting there grouching, it's brilliant.' (John, 19 years, Merseyside)

If the active elements of heroin's effects were open to a wide variety of forms of description and interpretation, these people were nevertheless in agreement that they liked the drug's effects. And another common feature in many of the accounts that we were given was the drug's capacity to take away a person's worries:

> 'I'd just finished with my girl . . . and I suppose I was on a bit of a downer myself like, a bit depressed and all that. And as I say I took some heroin, and all my worries that I had just seemed to float away . . . . When I had heroin, I didn't have a problem, I didn't have any worries.' (Paul, 24 years, Merseyside)

In many of the accounts that we were given an ambivalence surrounded descriptions of the drug's pleasures, which is hardly surprising since many of the people whom we talked to were trying to stay off heroin. Indeed, sometimes it was not easy to get people to talk about the enjoyable aspects of heroin use at all, in that they preferred to dwell upon the damage which heroin had caused in their lives. At one extreme, in an interview with a self-help group of ex-users (which we were not allowed to put on tape) the group leader vetoed any discussion of the pleasures of heroin at all. The group's philosophy involved a total renunciation of drug experiences, which is common to organisations such as Alcoholics Anonymous, and even to think about the pleasures of heroin was defined as a sign that a group member might relapse. And in a family interview in South Yorkshire something similar was at issue, so that when the interviewer asked what was so special about heroin for one moment a window was opened on the attractions of the drug, only to be quickly closed again:

> *Interviewer:* '*So what is it about heroin, compared to blow or speed or . . .?*'

> Cheryl: 'Y'know, heroin. It teks everything away, don't it?'

> Wendy: 'Oh aye. No worries . . .'

> Cheryl: 'You feel reet at ease, like, know what I mean, your mind's reet . . .'

> Mother: 'You were reet at ease when . . .[inaudible, everyone shouting at once] becomes one big worry, though, don't it!'

> Brother: 'Teks all yer worries away and then becomes a bigger one itsen.'

> Mother: 'Yeh, it does.'

> (Cheryl, 20 years; Wendy, 19 years; South Yorkshire)

This dynamic tension must be part of the daily life of many families who are trying to adjust to the problems caused by a member's heroin use. If Beckford's (1985) work on the experiences of the families of ex-Moonies can be used as a basis of comparison, then these tensions will often require an ex-addict to deny one side of their ambivalent feelings towards their past life. Given that denial is not the most helpful basis on which to come to terms with complex experiences and emotions, the family life of drug users is an area that would probably repay detailed consideration.

The early experiences of heroin use, from the accounts that we have been given, suffer from a wide variation. For some people the drug is an instant 'buzz' or 'hit'. For others

40

it is a matter of relaxation. For some it brings an enhanced sense of personal power. For others it means being 'wiped out' and 'wrecked'. But with different shades of emphasis, one common feature was the ambivalence felt towards the drug, while another was that heroin 'took your worries away' and made people feel 'at ease' with themselves and in their minds. Indeed, if anything it was this cushioning effect from external pressures which caused people to form an initial attachment to the drug and which then led them in to a regular pattern of consumption which eventually resulted in addiction.

On occasion, this feeling of release from external pressures and worries was so all-consuming in a person's recollections of their early heroin use that the positive drug effects (in the sense of a 'buzz' or a 'hit') were almost entirely absent from their account. And this seemed to be particularly so where someone's construction of the subjective meaning of their drug use was closely tied to their experiences of social deprivation. In other words, where heroin appeared to 'solve' a person's difficulties with housing, unemployment or low income.

This is how Linda and Brian, the married couple in their mid-twenties whom we have met before, chose to describe their early experiences of heroin use. It will be remembered that they had previously used 'speed' on an occasional basis, and that heroin had been introduced to them when there was no amphetamine sulphate locally available. As an opening gambit the interviewer had asked them how their heroin use had started, but the couple chose to answer in a roundabout way in which other concerns were to the forefront of their attention.

Interviewer: 'How did you get into heroin then?'

Linda: 'Oh, it were terrible.'

Brian: 'We lived in't front room . . . like it's knocked down now.'

Interviewer: 'Oh you weren't living here?'

Linda: 'No, another house.'

Brian: 'They knocked it down it were that bad. We ended up wi' . . . there were no gas, there were no watter, we had to go next door for us watter . . .'

Linda: 'Chimney fell down . . .'

Brian: 'Chimney fell in't back, and they wouldn't let us use gas fire, they wouldn't let us use it. So we got no gas, no electricity, nowt . . . And we were living in theer, and they were still wanting us to pay rent for it, wouldn't get us out or nowt.'

Interviewer: 'Who was that, the Council?'

Brian: 'Yeh. And we lost a young un through it like, Linda were pregnant and she lost a young un through it. After that, that's what did it weren't it, that's what started us?'

Linda: 'Yes.'

Brian: 'Too many problems and, like, we had some henry one day like, and we went back to't house, and we forgot all about house, because we were . . . you know . . . just didn't see nowt, so it were . . .'

Linda: 'That were it.'

Brian: 'Yeh, you see like, all't problems through house like. It were a shit tip weren't it?'

Linda: 'Yeh. It were terrible.'

Brian: 'Couldn't use upstairs cos all't rooves had fell in. And t'babby, me and our Linda used to sleep...'

Linda: 'We slept on... on a scatter cushion...'

Brian: 'We slept on one o' them us, on't floor. That were for twelve month that. And t'babby slept on't settee, didn't she?'

Linda: 'So that's what kept us into heroin that.'

Brian: 'Yeh.'

Linda: 'Because... it puts you, like, in Ethiopia at first...'

Brian: 'Yeh, it's like...'

Linda: 'Ethiopia!...[laughs]... Utopia... Utopia.'

Brian: 'It's just like, you just can't, you're just not bothered about nowt then. It's... great.'

(Linda and Brian, mid-twenties, South Yorkshire)

At first Linda and Brian had used heroin weekly, in the same way that they had previously taken amphetamine on an occasional weekend basis. But whereas their use of 'speed' had assumed a stable pattern of controlled use, they found that they were soon using heroin with increasing regularity. And what it offered this couple was not a 'buzz' or a 'hit', but an escape from their wretched housing problem. As they understood it, it was this which made their continuation of heroin use more likely once they had been offered it and tried it for the first time.

Quite apart from Linda's delicious confusion was to whether heroin had transported her into Ethiopia or Utopia — and maybe at a time when the Ethiopian famine was so much in the news her slip of the tongue betrayed its own set of meanings about a drug which could transform the nightmare of poverty (Ethiopia) into the land of milk and honey (Utopia) —her choice of words was very careful. Rather obviously this couple felt some close connection between their poverty and their heroin use. Nevertheless, Linda did not say, 'That's what caused it'. She said, 'That's what kept us into heroin'. And she is quite right. At this second vital transition point — from experimentation to a pattern of more regular use — what 'keeps' people into heroin is what matters, because they are not yet addicted. For some it is the pleasure — the 'buzz', the sense of power, the 'wrecked' feeling of 'gouching out'. For others it is the ability of heroin to 'solve' their problems, and to cushion them either from the world or from themselves.

The Question of Non-Addictive Occasional Use

If there is very little research on early patterns of heroin use, except as reconstructed from the experiences of addicts and ex-addicts, then the occasional user who only takes heroin on a recreational basis is even more elusive. Indeed, there are authoritative traditions within the addictions field which question whether heroin use is even possible without eventually becoming addicted. Nevertheless, a substantial body of research evidence on non-compulsive opiate use has been collected by Zinberg and his colleagues in the USA, where occasional heroin use on a recreational basis is known within the drug culture as 'chipping'. This has established beyond doubt that stable patterns of non-addictive heroin use can be sustained if certain rules are adhered to (cf. Zinberg,

1984). Zinberg's work, which contains a useful summary of research in this little explored area, had also attempted to identify what these rules, rituals and routines amount to. Briefly, the necessary underlying supports which can sustain a non-complusive pattern of opiate use include the following: access to a knowledgeable network of controlled drug users who can offer advice to the novice; strict adherence to rules on the frequency of use, so that the drug is only used on certain occasions such as at weekends and at no other time, and never on consecutive days; the existence of other valued commitments in a person's life such as employment, family life and recreational pursuits which conflict with opiate use; and a circle of friendship which includes non-users as well as users.

Other research confirms this general impression. Peele (1985) has advanced the view that the social-psychological basis of addictive experiences is more important than their physiological components, arguing that people become addicted to activities and not to substances. Compulsive behaviour, he points out, is sometimes associated with practices such as gambling, food intake, or even the pursuit of physical fitness. According to this view what distinguishes controlled opiate users from compulsive users is that they 'subordinate their desire for a drug to other values, activities and personal relationships, so that the narcotic or other drug does not dominate their lives. When engaged in other pursuits that they value, these users do not crave the drug or manifest withdrawal on discontinuing their drug use' (Peele, 1985, p. 8).

In Britain a smaller study by Blackwell (1984) identified similar features within the lifestyles of controlled opiate users, while also pointing to the way in which people sometimes move between different statuses of involvement with heroin. Blackwell's work has particular interest for its indications of how occasional users sometimes felt that their heroin use was drifting out of control towards dependence, whereupon they took action to regulate their involvement. The motivating factors which precipitated these moves include the following:

> 'Loss of appetite, irregular sleep patterns, needle marks and spotty complexions . . . .
> Two respondents said that they stopped using in order to get into shape for the
> football season.' (Blackwell, 1984, p 228)

What is remarkable about these accounts is that, given the common view of heroin as a totally enslaving preoccupation, such trite reasons as 'getting into shape for the football season' could trigger an exit-route towards abstinence. In more general terms, in fact, Blackwell's research confirms the view of Zinberg and Peele that for controlled opiate use to be sustained over time there must be other commitments in a person's life which compete with the claims of heroin.

Our research can neither confirm nor deny these impressions, in that we had no contact with people who could be categorised as 'occasional' heroin users. Nearly all our informants who had used heroin, with the exception of a small number who had only very briefly flirted with the drug, had developed a pattern of compulsive use in time. But this is hardly surprising in a research project such as ours, because it is likely that only long-term ethnographic fieldwork would be able to ferret out the much more elusive recreational heroin user who has not come to the notice of public authorities. Moreover, our research was carried out in towns and cities that are suffering from very high levels of unemployment, so that one major form of life commitment — namely, a work identity — was simply not available for many people. In which case the absence of occasional users could be taken to offer negative evidence for the Zinberg–Peele thesis: that without other sustaining commitments, heroin will quickly take over your life.

Our analysis of the Small Area Statistics of the 1981 Census confirmed that there was a correspondence between the existence of a serious heroin problem in those neighbourhoods which we studied and high densities of unemployment (see Appendix). In a major study from the 1960s of heroin use among juveniles in New York, it was also noted that those neighbourhoods where heroin use was most prevalent were economically deprived areas which were also characterised by a sense of futility which was thought to be conducive to experimentation with narcotics (Chein *et al.*, 1964). Moreover, under such circumstances being a heroin addict can itself be a means by which a person can establish an identity and claim status within the peer-group, something which was once more reflected in studies of New York and Chicago in the 1960s and early 1970s (Feldman, 1968; Hughes and Crawford, 1972; Fiddle, 1976; Hendler and Stephens, 1977).

This is not to advance a causal argument of the relationship between unemployment and heroin use — there are areas of high unemployment where there is not an extensive heroin problem, such as the North-East of England. But where there is both high unemployment and the easy availability of heroin within the friendship network, there seems to be an increased likelihood, as Chein and his colleagues suggested in their New York study, that people will experiment with heroin. And then, most crucially, more likelihood that excessive and uncontrolled patterns of heroin use will rapidly develop because of the absence of other commitments and viable alternatives through which to fashion self-esteem and a meaningful identity. The social psychology of employment and unemployment suggests that it is through a work identity that people gain access to a wider set of involvements, friendships and activities than would otherwise be the case. Employment status confers major elements of self-esteem, and it is also the basis of meaningful time-structures with a person's daily routines (cf. Jahoda *et al.*, 1972 edn; Jahoda, 1982).

These are precisely the forms of commitment which the available research on controlled opiate use suggests are necessary if a person is to sustain occasional non-addictive use over any length of time. If these forms of commitment are either absent or not valued, then according to the work of Zinberg, Peele and others, one would not expect to find stable patterns of recreational opiate use within a drug-using community. From South Yorkshire the mother of an ex-addict, Cheryl, offered an admirable commonsense view of the Zinberg–Peele thesis in the following terms:

> 'Don't you think you've got to put it this way. People what are working, if they've got good sense, they've got sommat good to look out for. They're not gonna tek it, are they, through't week when they're going to work. Where as you get somebody what's in't unemployed, they'll have it at weekend and they'll continue wi' it, cos they got nowt else to do, have they? Because you do get sensible people like that, don't you, if they're working they just . . . they'll not bother wi' it through't week. Well that's how I see it.'

In attempting to explain why patterns of occasional heroin use seemed to be largely unknown to our informants, another major consideration is the nature of the drug culture itself. Whereas in North America the phenomenon of 'chipping' is widely known, so that occasional opiate use is an available option within the repertoire of drug choices, our evidence suggests that in the working-class communities that we have studied this is not so. Some of our informants could think of people whom they had encountered and who appeared to be able to use heroin on a 'take it or leave it' basis, but they were essentially puzzled as to how this was possible. The heroin subculture to which they had been introduced only seemed to know and care about patterns of daily use. So that when asked about occasional users our informants would say that many people started off using heroin occasionally; but whereas they might believe at first that they could control the drug, if it were used daily for several weeks then addiction was inevitable. But this misses the point. No one has ever suggested that heroin can be used on a daily basis for any length of time without becoming addictive. The simple fact was that within the drug cultures that we encountered occasional use was not recognised as an option, nor for that matter desired. Novice heroin users were socialised into a drug culture that was devoted to daily use and getting 'wrecked' day in, day out. In this way the contemporary heroin subculture is similar to the reckless lifestyle of the 'chaotic' poly-drug user of London in the late 1970s where barbiturate injection was the most prevalent form of drug abuse (cf. Jamieson *et al.*, 1984). So that the prevailing drug culture, far from offering safeguards against high-risk forms of drug involvement in the way that the North American 'chipping' culture does, is an incitement to runaway heroin misuse on a daily basis. Taken together with the absent claims of an effective work commitment for so many people within these neighbourhoods, the specific form which the drug culture has assumed means that a pattern of occasional or recreational heroin use does not appear to be a real option as things stand.

Transitional Use: Mistaken Identities in the 'Grey Area'

Addiction does not follow on instantly from experimentation with heroin, and although the rate at which a person becomes addicted probably varies between individuals it will have been necessary to use the drug regularly on a daily basis for some time before the actual development of a 'habit'.

The transition into compulsive, addicted use is clearly an important change of status in the career of a heroin user, and it will often be characterised by an imperceptible drift —a 'grey area' where a person's growing involvement with heroin is unclear and open to misinterpretation. We can identify two kinds of such misinterpretation within this transition, each with its own attendant dangers. The first is where a person believes themselves to be addicted when in fact he or she is not. The second is when a person does not believe themselves addicted, when in fact he or she is.

The first case of mistaken identity is probably more common than is usually recognised. In one locality a drug squad officer reported to us that he had often noticed that people who had been arrested on drug charges did not exhibit any withdrawal symptoms when they were held in custody on remand, even though they believed themselves to be heroin addicts. His explanation of this phenomenon was that people who claimed to be heroin addicts when they were not were 'showing off' in front of their friends, and one thing which certainly has to be reckoned with is that in some localities being a 'smack head' is assuming something of a heroic status. However, this is not necessarily a conscious choice, and we can identify a number of subtle, interacting influences which play a part in these misrepresentations of self within the 'grey area' of transitional heroin use.

Perhaps the most important is that in the absence of a well-informed drug culture a person might be a victim of the mythology of heroin's 'instantly' addictive powers, and therefore pursue and consume the drug in fear of withdrawal before an actual physical dependence had been established. In a situation such as this a person's mistaken belief that he or she is addicted will quickly become a 'self-fulfilling prophecy', and a number of ex-users whom we talked to described in their own terms how these mistaken identities might arise and then lead eventually to addiction:

'I think people get the wrong ideas, you know, people who've just started on it ... and they've smoked it for a month or two months, and then they haven't got it one day. Well, all right, you know, they might feel a bit rough. But they start, y'know, they've got it in their heads that they're going through withdrawal symptoms. So they're out to get more to make them feel that bit better because they were feeling rough ... and before you know it, they *are* hooked on it.' (Paul, 24 years, Merseyside)

'When you get hooked on it you get, sort of, psychologically hooked at first. Do you know what I mean? You're saying, "I need this ... I need it", like ... and you don't.

But you buy it again, and then one day you just wake up and you're fucked.' (Eddie, 21 years, Merseyside)

An alternative set of reasons why people might embark upon a regular pattern of heroin use even before they become addicted, is that it gives them some meaning in life, either in the shape of an identity ('I'm an addict') or as status within the peer-group. One young man from Manchester described to us how when he first started using heroin, he enjoyed the notoriety which attached to it. 'People had to take notice of me, like. Suddenly I was someone round here . . . Jack the Lad . . . before that I'd been a nobody.' Auld *et al.* (1985) have also described how an assumed addict identity can give people not only local status, but also other forms of social-psychological reward in the shape of sympathy from one's family and friends. Declaring oneself to be a 'junkie', and thereby assuming a helpless victim status, might then be understood under the right circumstances as a form of 'attention-seeking'. It has been pointed out to us on more than one occasion that it is not unknown for a young offender to claim addict status when appearing before a Court, thereby hoping to secure a sentence which involves 'help' rather than 'punishment'.

As people become more deeply involved with a heroin-using network, they also become increasingly identified with group activities which centre on drug use. In order to gain acceptance within this group of acquaintances, it might then be necessary to magnify one's familiarity with heroin. Tall stories abound in drug-using circles about so-and-so who took twenty 'dikeys' at one go and really 'gouched out'; about how awful it was the other day when you were 'turkeying' and couldn't get a 'bag' anywhere; or how someone had escaped from the clutches of the law by 'legging it' when the drug squad appeared around the corner. Similar heroic tales have an important function within other subcultural contexts such as football hooliganism (cf. Marsh *et al.*, 1978) and they undoubtedly play a large part in a person's self-identification with a drug culture.

Equally important in this respect is that the life of the heroin user is an extremely active one. They need to be constantly on their toes—knowing who is who in the drugs scene; who sells the best 'bag' and where to buy it; how to avoid getting 'burned' by a dealer, and how to know the difference between brick-dust and the real thing; constantly hustling for the money for the next bag. In a study of street addicts in New York, Preble and Casey (1969) showed how this hectic cycle of activity could assume more importance in a person's life than the effects of the drug itself (cf. Auld *et al.*, 1984). This corresponds with the argument advanced by Peele (1985) that people become addicted to activities just as much as they become addicted to substances. And it also squares with the commonly reported experience by ex-users that 'staying off' heroin was much more difficult than 'coming off' the drug, because the day seems so empty without the drug and its associated flurry of activity.

One can see, then, that within the 'grey area' of transitional use there is ample scope for a person to adopt harmful self-identifications with the addict lifestyle prior to the actual onset of dependence, in such a way that these generate a 'self-fulfilling prophecy'. But it is equally true that a different kind of mistaken identity can be assumed, whereby addiction overtakes someone without them realising how deeply involved they have become with the drug. In some people's accounts of their transition into habitual use, their experience of how this came about was simply passed over in a sentence:

'I just got into it, buying a bag every day because I had money then, from the redundancy money and that, and before I knew it like, I was dependent on it . . . I needed it. (Malcolm, 23 years, Manchester)

Abbreviated recollections such as these are not terribly helpful if one is trying to reconstruct the pattern of transitional use, except perhaps as a warning of how rapidly and imperceptibly heroin addiction can sometimes be established. In all probability such accounts gloss over a range of decision points and choices that were made over time during this imperceptible drift.

We can trace some of the characteristics of the transition to habitual use through the experiences of two women from different parts of the North of England whose initial experiences of heroin were quite opposed, but who were both taken by surprise when they discovered that they developed withdrawal symptoms if they did not use the drug daily. Indeed, their surprise was so total that neither of them realised what these symptoms were when they first appeared.

Sharon is 21 years old and she first began using heroin four years ago, at a time when heroin was only just beginning to appear in her locality. Indeed, when Sharon and her girlfriend were first offered heroin by a friend, they did not even know what it was:

> 'When we first started taking smack there was none of these adverts or nothing like that, and it wasn't called "heroin", it was called "smack" . . . and it still is, like, but before it really started getting as it is now, it was just called smack. And a lad that we knew says to us, "Do you want some smack?" And we said [in a whisper] "What's that?" He says, "It's a substitute for heroin", or something, I can't really remember. And he said, "You can't get hooked on it" and that like. So we said, "All right then", and me and a friend had a bag between us. Well, we only had half the bag and we were wrecked . . . really stoned. We thought, "It's all right this". So we just went on for about two weeks solid, just buying bags, and we'd smoke that like . . . we must have done a terrible lot, and we were smoking a bag each then . . . Then after a solid month we started withdrawing. But when you first take smack and you're first withdrawing, you don't know what it is. Because as far as anyone knew you couldn't turkey off it. And I was just coming down with the shakes and all that . . . I thought I had the flu. And it wasn't until someone said to me, like "Oh you're withdrawing" . . . I nearly died of shame.' (Sharon, 21 years, Merseyside)

Whether or not it would have made any difference to Sharon's story if there had been an advertising campaign (or local knowledge) to warn of heroin's dangers is highly questionable, as we have seen from other people's accounts. In any case, in 1981 when she first tried heroin there was a sudden and dramatic alteration in the availability of the drug, as she recalled it, and the extent of its use:

> 'You'd go round and everyone was just into draw, [i.e. cannabis], and then when we were taking smack, just getting into it, there was a bit of it around, not much though. And then all of a sudden, everyone you met like, they'd go, "Such and such a person's a smack head now" . . . "God, is he?" . . . "Yeh". It just went round, like it seemed to get off in about two months. Everyone was on it. People I went to school with, who were really stuck up at school and that like, they were on it. It was just amazing, the people who were at it . . . It just come in all at once. It was hardly ever heard of, was it? It's really been in the last two years, something like that . . . There's that much demand for it now. I don't know how they'll stop it, though. Not unless they do something drastic because there's that much demand for it'.

Sharon is speaking here of a locality in which a heroin problem of truly epidemic proportions has established itself within the past few years, and which had penetrated deeply into local youth cultures. In the electoral ward where she lived unemployment was running at 35 per cent in 1981, and in the under-25 years age group it was substantially higher with small pockets of the area experiencing an unemployment rate of 60 per cent in this age group. Experience suggests that where heroin becomes available under such circumstances, then it can spread rapidly through a neighbourhood.

Sharon slipped into heroin use in her late teens, without any real knowledge of the drug she was using, and at a time when getting a 'buzz' off heroin was becoming fashionable among young people in her locality. In sharp contrast we can compare the experience of Josephine from another part of the North where heroin is much less widespread, who began using it two years ago when she was already 26 years of age and who had to overcome a great deal of initial reluctance before she would try the drug.

Unlike Sharon, Josephine had an extensive knowledge of the drugs scene which reached back to her early twenties, and for some years she had been accustomed to snort a line of 'speed' at the weekend with friends before going out for a night on the town. Her drug involvement had also brought her into contact with a few heroin users, whom she actually despised. Josephine was interested in music and dancing and having a good time at the pub or at a night club, whereas heroin users just sat around the house all day and did nothing. To this day she remains puzzled as to how she developed a heroin habit herself:

> 'I didn't think I would ever have got involved. I mean, I hated it. And I hated them too. And then when I did use it, how I got a habit I don't know, because for months it made me so ill . . . I just kept taking it.

> '*But why?*'

> 'I don't know, I just can't understand it myself. I suppose just because it was there . . . You see, I didn't think I had any problem with it because I didn't have to pay for it. Because my boyfriend's friends were all using it and that, and giving it to me . . . They were always offering me chases and at first I was refusing it, but then I gradually slipped into it. And then, as I say, one day I sort of realised that I'd had it every day for six days.'

By chance, it was just at this time that she had arranged to visit a friend in a distant town. And although by now she had been taking heroin regularly, it did not occur to her to take any with her, partly because she did not believe that she was addicted. She was away from home for three days, and Josephine noticed that she did not feel too well, but again it did not occur to her that this had anything to do with heroin: 'I just didn't feel myself . . . wound up, agitated, I just didn't feel well.' On her return journey home she began to feel poorly again, but still she did not make any connection between her symptoms and her heroin use. It was only when she had a 'chase' with some friends when she got home, whereupon her symptoms disappeared, that she realised what had happened:

> '*When you say you felt terrible, what did you feel like?*'

> 'Oh just absolutely useless . . . I had this craving as well, as I say I'd had it for six days constantly before I went away for a few days. But all the time I was away I just didn't feel . . . right . . . you know, I just didn't feel myself. I felt . . . wound up, agitated, and I just didn't feel well.'

> '*And you knew if you had some heroin it would bring you back to normal?*'

> 'Oh no. I didn't know, I didn't know that. In fact when I went round to those friends, I didn't go deliberately to get some heroin . . . In fact I think I went round to borrow a bottle of milk. You see I'd just got back and there was nothing in the house.'
> (Josephine, 28 years, Humberside)

Neither Sharon nor Josephine realised that they had developed an addictive pattern of heroin use until withdrawal symptoms appeared, and even then they had not realised at first that it was withdrawal they were suffering from. But in other respects their experience of heroin in the 'grey area' of transitional use was quite different. Sharon had first used the drug in the company of a girlfriend who was also a novice, and they had

48

immediately enjoyed the 'buzz'. In Josephine's case it had been within a circle of experienced heroin users whom she had actively disliked, and the drug continued to make her sick for some months. Sharon had to pay for the drug almost from the beginning, whereas Josephine had it on tap within her circle of friends and acquaintances. And whereas Sharon began using at a time when the habit was spreading rapidly among young people in her locality where it was associated with daring and excitement at first, Josephine lived in an area with a much smaller and less obtrusive heroin network which had settled into its reclusive and inward-looking routines of staying at home and doing little else. And then there was the question of age and experience. Sharon was not yet 18 years old when she first tried heroin, having accepted 'smack' on the first occasion that it was offered to her. Josephine was a woman of 26 years, with a respectable job, and she persistently refused offers of heroin for some months before she first accepted. But for all these initial differences, the subsequent careers were very similar, involving a rapid and imperceptible drift as they crossed the threshold of transitional use into addiction. Heroin, in this sense, can be a great leveller.

The impression that is so often given in these accounts of a heroin user's early experimentation and transition through the 'grey area' into addiction is one of inevitability. In retrospect, it no doubt feels as if the transition was inevitable. But the 'grey area' of transitional use does not necessarily take this form, and people can and do arrest their involvement and so avoid what would otherwise be the inevitable consequences of daily heroin use. So that whereas in Josephine's phrase, 'I just slipped into it', it is reasonable to suppose that over a period of weeks and months certain conscious choices and decisions were made. And also that these decisions would sometimes involve various kinds of subterfuge, by which people hide from themselves the obvious consequences of their actions. Perhaps the most common form which these subterfuges take is revealed in the often repeated expression, 'One little toot won't do me any harm', a self-deception whereby someone says to themselves that they will do it again today, but not tomorrow. And then when tomorrow comes, the same act of bad faith: 'One more little toot . . . Just one more little chase.'

One of the characteristics of accounts given by heroin users and ex-users is that they rarely embrace any recognition of their own motivation and agency. So that the drift into addiction is remembered only as something in which one played a passive role —as if the user were powerless in the face of a relentless pharmacological process, and then later driven by the overriding concern to avoid symptoms of withdrawal. But there is something highly dubious about accounts such as these. What one needs to ask, in a preliminary way, is what is it that is so overpowering and frightening about withdrawal symptoms which Sharon first mistook for a dose of the flu, and which Josephine endured for three days without realising that they had anything to do with heroin at all?

'Coming Off' and 'Staying Off'

Just as the experience of entry into heroin use can take different forms for different individuals, so the experience of coming off heroin can assume different meanings for different people. There are four major issues which emerge from our research.

(i)   'Withdrawal' can mean different things. Some heroin users describe it as a terrifying 'cold turkey'. But more commonly people describe it as no worse than a bad dose of influenza, and some people feel that the problems of withdrawal are not bodily at all but 'in your head'.

(ii) Coming off heroin can either be a once-and-for-all process, or it can involve a series of gradations: for example, from injecting to smoking, from smoking to methadone maintenance, from methadone maintenance to methadone reduction. Obviously, these paths are not taken entirely by freely determined individual choice, but also depend upon the patterns of specialist services available.

(iii) Coming off can either be assisted by professionals, most commonly in the form of a methadone reduction course, or it is something which people do on their own, with or without the support of family and friends. A number of people described to us how they had taken themselves on holidays, away from the area where heroin was available to them, in order to effect a withdrawal. But they also sometimes found that they relapsed when they returned to where they lived.

(iv) Whatever the experience, it is generally agreed that 'coming off' is one thing, but that the real problem is 'staying off'. Many of our informants had had the experience of coming off — sometimes for a period of months, but more commonly for a few weeks — and then slipped back into habitual use. These problems invariably centred on friendship networks where someone who had become abstinent still had many addict friends, together with the major difficulty of how to structure one's day in order to avoid boredom and apathy. And it is once again especially difficult for someone to know how to become involved in a wider set of acquaintances and activities in those areas which suffer from high levels of unemployment.

The actual decision to 'come off' can often be quite sudden, and this has important implications for service delivery. The experience of London street agencies studied by Dorn and South (1985) is that drug users who are not motivated to come off nevertheless have a variety of unmet needs, such as housing difficulties, problems with their social security payments, domestic and family problems, etc. These needs are not strikingly different from those of the non-drug-using clientele of social workers and probation officers. On the basis of this London experience it would seem to be a mistake for services to be geared solely towards counselling a drug user to come off drugs when that person has not yet discovered the self-motivation. If an unmotivated drug user has used an agency periodically for help with other matters, such as housing and social security problems, then a basis of trust will have been established. This trust may be developed over many months of offering friendship and advice to an unmotivated drug user over a variety of problems, and can then be the foundation for prompt and effective help if and when that person discovers the motivation to do something about the drug problem (Dorn and South, 1985, p. 60).

If this might be considered as an ideal model, then the actual experience can be quite different. June, for example, was a woman in her early-twenties who had been regularly using heroin for six months when an ex-boyfriend who had been working abroad wrote to say that he was coming home. She had been very fond of him, and this was her initial motivation to stop using heroin before his return. She went to see her general practitioner who told her that he had no experience of heroin addiction and that he could only arrange an appointment for her to attend a local clinic in six weeks' time. June's boyfriend was due home in a month, and dispirited by this response she continued to use heroin daily and did not get herself to the clinic.

Colin, on the other hand, did manage to sustain his motivation until the time of a clinic appointment when he was given a routine urine analysis and told to come back in four days. He failed to meet this second appointment, but phoned the clinic on the following day to ask if he could be seen after the weekend. Having been told that it was clinic policy that if you failed an appointment then you went to the back of the queue, which involved waiting for another month, he took himself off to see his family doctor immediately:

'He told me he couldn't do nothing for me, 'cos now I was under the clinic like. I got really mad, shouting at him and all that, and we had a bad argument me and the doctor. I remember, I pulled this money out of my pocket and waved it at him . . .

50

like, "Look, I could go and buy smack now, like, but I don't want it, I want some methadone to help me get off". I wanted to get off it like. When he got it into my head that he couldn't do nothin' for me, and that I had to wait another month like . . . well, I thought "Fuck it, I'll do it on me own" like. And I did, and I've never bothered with clinics or nothin' since.' (Colin, 22 years, Merseyside)

Having discovered the motivation to 'come off' and carried this motivation through, what is the actual experience of withdrawal? We noted in our description of the pleasurable effects of heroin that it is often difficult for people to say what these are and that their accounts vary. Equally, the experience of withdrawal can be difficult for heroin users to put across, and it is also described in different terms by different people. This may be because the experience is actually different for different people, with some suffering more severe physical reactions than others. But what is certain is that the common stereotype of 'cold turkey' as a horrifying experience that is beyond the extremities of ordinary understandings of pain is not always shared by heroin users who have gone through the experience of withdrawal.

'Is it as bad as they make out?'

'No, I don't think so. It's bad, really, but you can't explain it like. It's hard to explain what a turkey is, like . . . . A lot of people say that this happens and that happens, but when I done my turkey it wasn't as bad as I was expecting. But it was bad, if you know what I mean . . . It was unbearable, like, but it wasn't as bad as I was expecting.' (Eddie, 21 years, Merseyside)

'So apart from those times when you've been off it for a couple of months, have you ever tried coming off again?'

'Er, quite a few times I've come off it for like seven days, I haven't touched it for seven days, but gone back on it. It's not the actual coming off, you know this thing you hear, "cold turkey" and all that . . . . That's, most of it's in your head, you know, mental, memory sort of thing . . . I think people get the wrong ideas.' (Paul, 24 years, Merseyside)

'What do you reckon about withdrawals then?'

'Well, it's the hardest thing in my life that I've ever had to go through. Hardest thing like, I feel reet sorry for people, now me . . . I still do off methadone, I still withdraw off methadone. 'Cos like that's just same as heroin isn't it? . . . Well, it in't but . . . . One time he [the psychiatrist] cut me down too much, and I couldn't do it, I couldn't manage with what he were geeing me . . . and I were dying . . . well, I weren't but . . .' (Cheryl, 20 years, South Yorkshire)

'As soon as you wake up it's like a ton of bricks coming down on you, "Where am I going to get my money from today?". But like, when you think about it now, most of it is psychological. Like you wake up and you think, "I should be turkeying" and that, but you're not turkeying. "I should be turkeying, what's going on?" . . . I wouldn't say, like, you can just forget about it, going for a walk, it's not like that. I'm saying like, you wake up in a morning . . . like I think everyone gets up in a morning and they start turkeying, it's natural isn't it? But you wake up and you're feeling all right and you think, "I should be turkeying" . . . But I wouldn't say it was easy . . .' (Sharon, 21 years, Merseyside)

These accounts of withdrawal experiences are full of ambiguity. But this is not because the individuals themselves are inarticulate. Rather, there would seem to be some inherent difficulty in describing the internal states associated with both the effects of heroin and withdrawal from it. Faced with these difficulties, the heroin user will sometimes resort to the stereotype of the horrors of withdrawal, although even then they will cover their tracks by an explicit disclaimer: 'I were dying, well I weren't, but . . .'; 'It was unbearable, like, but it wasn't as bad as I was expecting.'

Excessive fears of withdrawal can undoubtedly act as a discouragement to a heroin user who might be thinking of trying to come off heroin, just as they sometimes acted as an encouragement for people to continue using the drug in the early stages of transitional use. For these reasons it would seem important for health education purposes that this stereotype of 'cold turkey' is corrected by more accurate information that is faithful to the experience. And the more faithful record of these experiences is that it is possible to come off heroin, and that it is not the total enslavement that it is often imagined to be. But having said that, when someone has come off heroin the real problem is to stay off, and this is far more difficult.

The pressures of friendship networks are a major obstacle to staying off heroin, where a person's friends are still using it and the drug is easily available. But people also describe how their lives seem so empty after they have come off, and speak of the need to get involved with things again. But how to do this is easier said that done:

> 'It just seems the hardest thing in the world to stay off smack . . . like I say, I've been off it a week, more than a week, but you just go back on it 'cos it's round here, you know. . . . I think, like, unemployment and that has got a lot to do with it . . . with nothing to do, I'm sitting here, like, doing nothing . . . I'm bound to start thinking of smack again. And I'll probably feel down and all that like. And I'll probably go out and get smack. But like I'm determined this time, I've gotta get off it. Because it's fucked all my life up completely . . .'

> *'What kinds of things can you do to help then?'*

> 'That's what I'm trying to do, like, do at the moment. Graham [probation officer] he's helping me a bit like, he's trying to talk me into getting a job. But then there's no fucking jobs round 'ere, are there? But, no, be fair, Graham's all right and he's, like, trying to make me get up off my arse and do something. But at the moment, I don't really know from now on like, I don't know what's gonna happen. I want a job, like, I want to try and live . . . It's gonna be hard, like.' (Jack, 22 years, Merseyside)

Paul was another young man who offered a particularly rich account of the difficulties of coming off and staying off heroin. In his view, as we have already seen, the experience of withdrawal was vastly overrated. The real problem for him was 'not the coming off, it's the actual staying off that's the hardest thing'. First, he described what withdrawal might amount to:

> 'As I say, you're not really . . . you're only . . . your first four days are pretty bad, you know, you get the flu symptoms, you sweat, and you can't sleep for the first three or four nights, you get diarrhoea, your legs are weak . . . But then after that, the four days, five days, you're on the up then. After a week, ten days . . . you just feel clean in yourself. You know what I mean, you feel the benefit sort of thing. But that's where your willpower comes into it. You know, you keep thinking to yourself, "By this time next week I'll be laughing" sort of thing. That's where a lot of people don't . . . er, after they've done it for two days, they haven't slept, they feel bad . . . before you know it they're up and out, they want some smack to get rid of it . . . But if you just stick at it, you can come off it. As I say, a lot of it's in the head. You know, you hear all these people talking about "cold turkey" and all this, well it's not that much.' (Paul, 24 years, Merseyside)

52

But if Paul took the view that it was not too difficult to come off with the application of some willpower (and he also acknowledged that he had received invaluable help from his family, by actively encouraging him to stick at it, and by tolerating his behaviour in the early stages of withdrawal) he was under no illusions about the difficulties of staying off. First there was the problem of changing your daily routines and avoiding contacts with the heroin scene:

> 'Getting out of the little rut you've been in for the last, y'know, twelve months or whatever... you know, getting up in the morning, going down for your gear, smoking the gear, what have you... It's just the actual boredom, you know, sitting in the house... like when I do come off, I just stay in the house. If anyone knocks I tell my mam to tell them I've gone to my sisters, just hibernate sort of thing. It's just getting through the day... I know if I go out I'll either meet someone round the area, 'cos everyone I know is on the heroin... there's still mates who are not on heroin, but because I've been on heroin, you know, we've just drifted apart. So anyone I go and meet is on heroin, and before I know it I'm back smoking myself again.'

Paul entertained ideas about 'getting involved with things, voluntary work, that sort of thing, talking to addicts and helping them like through your experiences'. But he also felt that there was something in the contrasts of experience between being on heroin and being off it which made it particularly difficult to stay off. Being on heroin for him meant that 'all my worries that I had just seemed to float away'. But after getting through withdrawal he found that the painful realisation of what he had been doing to himself, and to other people, began to crowd in upon him and Paul found this strain difficult to bear. Heroin, as he described it, was 'an emotional drug' and this made staying off all that more difficult:

> 'It's not until you're actually off the gear, and you've been off the gear a couple of weeks, that you realise. And you know, it really knocks you sick what you've been doing. It's an emotional drug, you know what I mean, it is a very emotional drug. You know, when you're coming off and you've been off the gear for a week or something, you're in the house with your family and all that, and you realise what you've done in the past, y'know, to get money and that, tricked them, lied and stole and all that. Well it upsets you like.'

And later in the interview, Paul returned to the theme:

> 'You have to sort of start your life again, put a lot behind you. There's a lot of things, like, that I've done that'll always be on my conscience. You know, like bad things I've done, tricks I've played, who I've stole off, and who I've lied to, and who I've hurt. And like, they'll be on my mind, psychological, for a long time. So it's not just the effect of going through your withdrawal and coming off the gear. You've got to get over emotional strains and things like that, you know, things that you try and forget about. But no matter how hard you try to forget them, they're still there. You know what I mean? You've still done them. And there's no way you can make up for some of the things that you've done. Unless, as I say, people forgive and forget.'

And one way that you could forget, as Paul's own experience of the cycle of abstinence and relapse had shown, was to go back on heroin.

Different people had tried different strategies by which to overcome these difficulties of restructuring the day and dealing with the painful emotions which began to flow again once they had become abstinent. Some people advocated the occasional use of 'speed' to help pass the day, although they sometimes recognised its own dangers. Others felt that smoking cannabis was a useful relaxing drug. Stimson and Oppenheimer (1982) also found that immediately following withdrawal from heroin people not uncommonly slipped into a pattern of heavy and problematic drinking for a few months, but that although very few ex-users continued to use other drugs in a potentially harmful fashion they sometimes found that either alcohol or cannabis subsequently proved useful in coping with their mental state. In our own study, where people lived in a locality where heroin was in plentiful supply there appeared to be essentially no strategies for 'coming off' that were entirely risk-free. Those people who had taken themselves off for holidays in order to 'come off' soon found when they returned that their abstinence was a fragile vessel. And the same was true for those who had entered in-patient detoxification programmes. Indeed, one young man had some sharp words when he was asked whether he had ever thought of going away to a local hospital which offered a methadone-reduction course:

> 'I wouldn't go there. I don't want to go away anywhere either to get off it. I'd rather stay around the area and get off it. 'Cos, like, you're gonna have to live in the area aren't yer? So you might as well do it where yer are, like.'

> *'So Phoenix house wouldn't suit you?'*

> 'No. I've got to do it off my own. Stay round where yer are and get off it. If you can't do that, like, stay in the area and beat it, you're never gonna get off it.' (Eddie, 21 years, Merseyside)

But then Eddie had a particularly robust view of where the responsibility for heroin abuse lay. We have mentioned the common tendency for heroin users to disown their own actions and motivations, and to speak as if they were passive victims within a relentless pharmacological process. Eddie did not see it that way at all, and he deserves to have the last word:

> 'There's no one to blame for it. It's yourself. You're the one that decides to get into it, so it's on your plate. It was no one's fault. I just got into it. It was sheer, "Oh that's nice" like, "I'll get into that" like . . . I've said to you before, it's no one's to blame. It's you. You're the one that's saying "Yeh!" If yer can say no, well fair enough, you're laughing aren't ya? If you can't say no, it's just hard shit. I'm not blaming no one for my addiction, it's my own fault like. I accept that.'

6 SUMMARY AND CONCLUSIONS

The aim of this final section is to summarise the contents of this report, and to say something about the social contexts within which health education must operate.

Local Variations and 'At Risk' Groups

A major finding of the research is the highly scattered and localised nature of heroin misuse at the moment. The uneven geographical distribution of heroin misuse is confirmed by other research studies in London (O'Bryan, 1985) and in the Wirral area of Merseyside (Parker *et al.*, 1986). In our own research it was found that heroin misuse tended to be more of a problem to the west of the Pennines than to the east of the Pennines. However, even within a town or city where there was a heroin problem, we found that this was itself subject to further local variation. So that although individual heroin users might be identified across a wide geographical area, the most serious pockets of misuse tended to be densely focused in certain neighbourhoods and not in others.

This localisation also extends to the style of heroin use that is prevalent in any given area, particularly whether the drug will be smoked or injected. A key issue in determining whether smoking or injecting technologies prevail within a locality appears to be the pattern of amphetamine usage which might have been established prior to the appearance of heroin in the North of England in the early 1980s. So that where amphetamine ('speed' or 'whizz') had been previously injected within the local drug subculture, then it is highly likely that heroin would also be injected when and if it became available within the locality. Whereas if injection techniques had not been locally established in such a way, then it would be more likely that heroin would be smoked on foil — 'chasing' or 'tooting'. Even so, within a given locality where the dominant preference is injecting, individuals will sometimes exercise a preference for smoking, and vice versa. It is also true that some individuals who begin smoking the drug move on from 'chasing' to injecting because this is a more efficient, and hence less costly, method of use. However, this is not a universal pattern as has been sometimes supposed. Indeed, there is no such thing as a universal style of heroin use, and health education practices need to be based on a sound understanding of local conditions.

Local variations in the extent of heroin misuse are in all probability determined by a number of factors. The most fundamental is whether a distribution network had been established, and hence whether the drug is simply available within a locality. One vital social factor which was identified in our research is that, although heroin misuse can become a problem for people from any class or background, there is a clear relationship between the severity of a local heroin problem where the drug has become available and various indicators of social deprivation such as unemployment levels. This link between illicit drug use and unemployment has been confirmed in other recent research studies, both in Scotland (Plant *et al.*, 1985) and Merseyside (Parker *et al.*, 1986). A summary of Census statistics which illustrate these links in those neighbourhoods studied in our research is to be found in the Appendix to this report.

Age is another important consideration in terms of whether people are most 'at risk' in relation to heroin use. There has been a large amount of publicity in recent months about very young heroin users in their early teens, and it seems to be assumed that it is this age group who are most at risk. However, although cases of school-age heroin users can be identified, they appear to be wholly exceptional even in localities with an epidemic heroin problem. The age group most at risk are young people in their late teens and early twenties, although there are also local variations in the age distribution of the heroin problem, and in some areas an older group in their mid-twenties were identified by professionals as the most common heroin users. Great care must be exercised in interpreting judgements such as these, however, because the 'hidden figure' of unknown heroin users who have not yet come to the notice of public agencies are likely to be younger than those who are known to professional and voluntary bodies. We can be quite sure, however, that among school-age youngsters the most common drugs of misuse are likely to be solvents, tobacco and alcohol. Whereas among an older population, agencies dealing with drug-related problems commonly report that the largest number of self-referrals are in connection with medically prescribed tranquillisers.

Variations in Agency Responses and Inter-Agency Conflicts

In addition to the local variations described above, different public agencies also have widely varying perceptions of the heroin problem. Even in an area with a serious problem of heroin misuse, this tends to make quite different impacts on the routine workloads of agencies, such as the Probation Service or Social Services Departments, whose work and typical clientele are otherwise very similar. Among non-specialist agencies such as these it is the Probation Service which seems to have most contact with heroin users or ex-users, and the best chance of a good local understanding. Social workers in Social Services Departments, by contrast, find that heroin-related problems make much less of an impact upon their routine workloads, and then most typically in the context of a childcare enquiry where one of the child's parents might be found to be using heroin. Community health service personnel, such as health visitors, seem to have even less contact with the problem or knowledge about heroin use locally. Similarly, Education Departments reported almost universally that heroin use was not considered to be an issue in the schools (although other drugs might be) so that even in areas with a major heroin problem it is a very rare occurrence for schools to become involved (cf. Parker *et al.*, 1986).

It is equally important to recognise that for different agencies a range of different demands are made on their time in connection with a wide range of different drugs, so that there are wide variations in the priorities which agencies give to different substances of misuse. This can sometimes make for real difficulties in establishing effective inter-agency collaboration in response to drug problems. Conflicts between agencies because of the ways in which different drugs make varying impacts on their routine workloads should not be underestimated in attempts to fashion drug liaison initiatives. It is perhaps better to identify these potential conflicts at the outset, rather than placing the initial emphasis on 'cooperation'. Effective cooperation will often be difficult to secure because of quite rational reasons, such as the different agencies' tasks and responsibilities, resulting in different preoccupations and priorities. We were able to identify a number of potential and actual conflicts between different agencies and professionals, as well as between these and the perceptions of members of the public, voluntary bodies, self-help groups and parents' groups.

Different policies are also pursued by specialist agencies in different localities, which makes it very difficult to offer generalised advice about available services to drug users and their families. There is no uniformity in terms of the availability of methadone maintenance, for example, and whereas in some areas this is an available treatment stratgegy, in others it is not and treatment facilities are aimed towards more or less immediate abstinence. There are also variations in local styles of policing in relation to drug problems, with public complaints in some areas that the police seem unconcerned about locally-based small-time user-dealers and more preoccupied with major traffickers. The policy pursued by specialist agencies (i.e. the police and the medical profession) can have important consequences in determining not only the availability of services, but also the local pattern and availability of drugs.

Different localities have also thrown up varying patterns of voluntary effort. In some areas there are active self-help groups, parent groups and other forms of community support groups, as well as attempts to develop inter-agency drug liaison initiatives which incorporate voluntary effort. However, in other areas these are not so well developed, and differences also exist in terms of the aims and methods of self-help and liaison activity. These differences are sometimes shaped by the local pattern of drug availability and drug problems. There are also significant ideological differences, such as whether the aim is to offer help and support to users and their families, whether or not a person is prepared immediately to discontinue drug use. Or whether the aim is to offer information and assistance to the police on drug-dealing networks. These two activities are not easily reconciled, because where a local group is known to be close to the police then they can quickly lose the trust of illicit drug users and their families.

Health Education Issues

These local variations — both in terms of the drug problems encountered in a locality and the nature of both statutory and voluntary agency responses — have important consequences for health education. It is difficult to see, for example, how a nationally devised strategy can in itself respond meaningfully and effectively to these wide local variations, whereby different localities face not only different problems but must also draw upon different patterns of local resources. Rather, what seems to be needed is a health education framework which can be closely tailored to local needs and resources. A similar recognition informed the inter-departmental government circular on *Crime Prevention* issued in January 1984 by the Home Office, DHSS, DES, DOE and Welsh Office which recommended highly focused and locally-devised crime prevention schemes adapted to locally-defined problems as the basis for effective multi-agency work (cf. Home Office, 1984). Given that heroin use is both a health risk and an illegal activity, then a comparable localised prevention strategy such as this might repay careful consideration.

Another major issue for health education is whether to aim for an outright preventive strategy which hopes to reduce the demand for drugs, or to provide 'harm-minimisation' advice whereby those who use drugs can be helped to reduce the health risks of drug misuse by avoiding the most harmful practices (cf. ACMD, 1984). 'Harm-minimisation' strategies are sometimes confused with condoning drug misuse, a viewpoint commonly found among parent groups whom we contacted during our research, and where the attitude towards 'harm-minimisation' could be exceptionally hostile. Professionals are sometimes reluctant to be associated with 'harm-minimisation' strategies for this reason, even though they recognise the potential value of such advice for drug users who might otherwise be more deeply injured by their drug misuse. Since the completion of our fieldwork the question of 'harm-minimisation' health education has been highlighted by the risk of AIDS through drug users sharing needles, although it is interesting to note that this was already rumoured to be a risk by some heroin users whom we interviewed in the summer of 1985. Moreover, it has long been recognised that a major risk of needle-sharing among drug injectors is hepatitis infection and yet this has never received anything like the same emphasis in public coverage of the hazards of heroin use. Of course, it would be unrealistic to expect that the risk of infection, either by hepatitis or AIDS, will reduce the extent of heroin use. However, this would be to misunderstand the object of 'harm-minimisation' education which, in the context of injection techniques, is to inform those at risk how to avoid the more harmful practices, such as sharing needles, injecting substances that are not designed to be injected, etc. Because local drug subcultures will vary in terms of the sophistication of their knowledge about injection techniques, this once more suggests the need for a localised approach to 'harm-minimisation' strategies as well as outright 'preventive' campaigns.

The question of injection techniques is only one of a number of issues that might be usefully addressed through health education programmes directed towards existing heroin users. Others might be education about the unpredictable outcomes of drug 'cocktails', or what appear to be the high risks associated with some drugs such as Palfium, which has become subject to wider misuse in some localities since the decreased availability of Diconal on prescription, which was a high-preference drug for some opiate misusers. 'Harm-minimisation' might also be directed towards the aim of assisting drug users to stabilise their pattern of drug misuse, or to substitute a less harmful practice for a more harmful one — for example, by smoking heroin rather than injecting it. In many quarters, as already noted, such aims would be defined as scandalously 'soft' on drug misuse, and they might be impossible to implement for this reason. Nevertheless, these examples serve to show that health education on drug questions is more complex than simply urging people to say, 'No'. At the very least, it seems important to encourage a wider and more open public debate on different health education strategies, including 'harm-minimisation' approaches, so that various policy options might be examined on merit for different target audiences.

Different Targets and Audiences: De-Mythologising Heroin

Although it might be possible to combine different bodies of information and skill enhancement within a single health education framework, to be used in different ways with different audiences, it is clear that there are a number of separate targets for health education on drug choices. Most obviously, these include the following: various professional audiences; the parents of drug users and those most likely to participate in voluntary groups; drug users themselves; and finally those who do not use heroin, but who might be considered to be at risk. One important unifying theme in health education for all these different audiences, however, must be a clearer understanding of what heroin use actually amounts to.

A great deal of mythology surrounds illicit drug use, and heroin especially is a drug that is shrouded in a number of powerful myths. These are often quite false to the actual experiences of heroin use, and they are therefore not conducive to credible health education practices. We shall very briefly examine a number of these in the following sections: the 'pusher' and the context of friendship in the distribution of heroin; the idea

58

of heroin as instantly addictive; the denial of pleasure in discussions of opiate dependence; and the horrors of withdrawal and 'cold turkey'.

The profits to be made in the commanding heights of the heroin economy are truly fantastic, thus attracting quite understandably a large amount of public attention on large-scale heroin traffickers and 'pushers' as a major public enemy. However, the role of the 'pusher' in encouraging someone to begin using heroin is vastly inflated and quite false to the actual circumstances in which someone is most likely to be introduced to the drug. For health education purposes it would be more advisable, and indeed more accurate, to highlight the context of friendship within which heroin changes hands at its lowest level of distribution — which is where the novice will be offered heroin, if at all. The initial offer of heroin and early experimentation with the drug — and both are still a comparative rarity in most parts of Britain today — will be among friends. If the object of preventive campaigns is to encourage people to say 'No', then it would seem vitally important that they should know what it is that they will be required to say 'No' to: and it will be to the gift of a friend, and not to the wiles of a stranger or a 'pusher'.

The idea that heroin is instantly addictive is also unhelpful and potentially harmful, in that it might lead to a 'self-fulfilling prophecy' in someone who was experimenting with the drug. It will also be counter-productive among groups of people who are experimenting with heroin and who have established a routine of occasional heroin use on a recreational basis, for the simple reason that they will have discovered from their own experience that the drug does not produce immediate enslavement, with the likelihood that this might discredit all health education advice. A more appropriate response to someone in this position might be an offer of 'harm-minimisation' advice on how to limit one's involvement with heroin, possibly through the observance of strict rules for use (cf. Zinberg, 1984). However, as noted in an earlier section, this is a highly contentious issue in that there is far from universal agreement that the stabilisation of patterns of drug use is a legitimate goal for health education, with a strong lobby seeing the only proper and effective aim as eventual abstinence. It could be argued against this, nevertheless, that it is a matter of emphasis and that stabilisation is a better platform from which to move towards abstinence than an escalating heroin habit which is a likely occurrence if a person does not understand the basis of controlled intoxicant use, and an inevitable outcome if they indulge in opiate use on a daily basis for any length of time.

A heroin habit is sometimes known in street slang as 'the monkey on your back', with the implication that heroin use is merely a burden with no attendant pleasures or satisfactions. Such a view often predominates in the accounts of heroin dependence given by successfully rehabilitated ex-addicts, and it is an understandable emphasis from someone who might have had to struggle hard in order to overcome a self-destructive habit and to remain abstinent from opiates. Nevertheless, such accounts fail to acknowledge the attractions of heroin and must therefore be suspect for credible health education purposes in that they do not address significant dimensions of the experience of heroin use. Heroin does not only produce extremely pleasurable and reassuring effects in those who take it, which is precisely why opiate use is attractive to some people, but the daily life of a heroin user involves its own excitements and achievements in the effort to 'score' successfully a reliable quantity and quality of the drug (cf. Preble and Casey, 1969; Johnson et al., 1985; Auld et al., 1984; 1985). The constant daily hustle brings an effective time-structure into the person's routine, which leaves a vacuum when a person is attempting to 'come off' and 'stay off' heroin: probably one of the major difficulties to be overcome if rehabilitation is to be successful. Perhaps the most misleading aspect of heroin's powerful mythology is that it is a pharmacological enslavement—the 'monkey on your back' — which sustains the drug's hold over people, while neglecting both the real pleasures and excitements which are its positive attractions.

The process of withdrawal from heroin, commonly known as 'cold turkey', is also surrounded by powerful myths. There can be no doubt that coming off heroin can be an unpleasant experience. However, heroin users commonly report that the experience of withdrawal is no worse that a bad dose of influenza for a few days, and that the real problem with heroin is not 'coming off' but 'staying off'. Some ex-users undoubtedly help to reinforce the view that 'cold turkey' is beyond the normal extremities of human pain, and it is likely that individual responses to opiate withdrawal do differ. Nevertheless, the more general support for the 'cold turkey' portrayal of horrifying pain is to be found once more in the ex-addict's self-dramatisation of his or her life experience: the 'I've been to hell and back' syndrome, as it was described to us by one ex-user. Focusing on the pains of withdrawal is something which might be thought of as useful for a preventive campaign aiming to deter potential users. However, it is not helpful for health education directed towards the rehabilitation of people who are using heroin and who wish to become abstinent. Indeed, it is likely to have the effect of deterring them from attempting withdrawal because of the fear of 'cold turkey'. What is needed is realistic advice on the likely effects of withdrawal, together with suggestions on how these effects can be ameliorated in order to ease the transition of detoxification. Among those self-help groups whom we contacted, some had rejected the self-dramatised ex-addict stance and adopted a low-key approach which offered simple reassurance that withdrawal was an achievable objective, offering mutual support in the face of the undeniable discomforts of withdrawal, and then in order to accomplish the more protracted task of 'staying off'.

The various myths which surround heroin and other 'hard' drugs are by no means new, and they have sometimes involved astonishingly improbable claims (cf. Musto, 1973). Our discussion certainly does not exhaust the different ways in which heroin's powerful mythology can distort our understanding, and hence limit our ability to intervene meaningfully, both in order to attempt to prevent more widespread drug misuse and to ameliorate the harm caused by that drug misuse which already exists. Nevertheless, these examples give some indication of how health education needs will differ widely across the spectrum of drug involvement, from the non-user through to someone who has developed a dependence on heroin. In the main body of the report, in the chapter on 'Becoming a Heroin User', we outline a simple four-phase model which describes different statuses of involvement with the drug: the non-user; the initial offer and experimentation; occasional use; compulsive use. Each different *status* can be thought of as a different *audience,* with varying health education needs. The passage between these different statuses describes *transition points* in a heroin user's career, which could be vital targets for health education which is designed to arrest a person's further and deeper involvement with the drug. Each status of involvement will also imply quite different possible *exit-routes* towards abstinence, with different windows of opportunity and also different obstacles to overcome. Effective health education will need to engage with all the various levels of this hierarchy of drug involvements, and not only with the bottom rung of prevention where the non-user meets with the initial offer. The form of distribution of heroin at its lowest level, which is the means by which new users are recruited, is within neighbourhood and friendship networks. Therefore, by attending to the health education needs of existing users as well as non-users, with the initial aim of enabling them to stabilise what could otherwise be an escalating habit, could also be a way of reducing one possible site of 'contagion' within a local network (cf. Hughes and Crawford, 1972) thus contributing to an overall preventive strategy. Similarly, friendship will often be an important stimulus in the development of a heroin user's motivation to 'come off' the drug, and it is therefore vital that friends and relatives should also have access to reliable information on the likely effects of withdrawal and how these might be ameliorated. Across a range of issues, it serves no useful purpose for the public to be informed only by the demonic mythology of heroin misuse. A recent parliamentary committee has described drug misuse as 'the most serious peacetime threat to our national well-being' (Home Affairs Committee, 1985), and however overstated this might be, it registers well enough the heightened levels of public anxiety at the moment. In which case, it seems important that we should have a wide-ranging, open and well-informed public debate on these issues, rather, as is so often the case, than remaining locked in the heroin mythologies of the past.

APPENDIX I:
HEROIN AND UNEMPLOYMENT: A NEIGHBOURHOOD ANALYSIS OF 1981 CENSUS SMALL AREA STATISTICS

In the table below each named locality (Moorside, Closefields, etc.) refers either to a specific neighbourhood or electoral ward. Each 'target area' refers to a sub-locality within that neighbourhood or ward where a specific heroin network was at its highest density. The statistical evidence, generated from the Enumeration District level of the Small Area Statistics of the 1981 Census, shows a gathering concentration of social deprivation within each Target Area.

	Unemployment[a]	Unemployment under 25 years[a]	One-parent families[b]	No access to car
Greater Manchester				
Moorside	24%	28%	31%	69%
Target area	33%	45%	31%	72%
Closefields	33%	40%	39%	74%
Target area	40%	66%	45%	84%
Greenleigh	23%	30%	29%	62%
Target area	36%	46%	34%	73%
Merseyside				
Docktown ward	34%	40%	24%	78%
Target area	53%	60%	38%	92%
South Yorkshire				
Steelborough	29%	35%	30%	65%
Target area	44%	47%	36%	74%

[a] All unemployment rates refer only to male unemployment. Female unemployment statistics tend to under-estimate the extent of unemployment because of non-registration.

[b] 'One-parent families' refers to the statistics in Table 31 of the 1981 Census. In Table 27 another estimate of single-parent households is offered which described those households with children and one 'lone adult'. Table 27 gives a substantially lower estimate on all counts, but Table 31 is generally thought to offer the better estimate because it includes also single parents who might share a household with kin, other families or friends.

BIBLIOGRAPHY

Advisory Council on the Misuse of Drugs, *Prevention* (HMSO, 1984).

Association of the British Pharmaceutical Industry, *Data Sheet Compendium, 1974* (ABPI, 1974).

J. Auld, N. Dorn and N. South, 'Heroin Now', *Youth and Policy*, vol. 2, no. 4, 1984.

J. Auld, N. Dorn and N. South, 'Irregular Work, Irregular Pleasures: Heroin in the 1980s', in R. Matthews and J. Young (eds.), *Confronting Crime* (Sage, 1985).

H.S. Becker, *Sociological Work* (Allen Lane, 1970).

J.A. Beckford, *Cult Controversies: The societal response to the new religious movements* (Tavistock, 1985).

J.S. Blackwell, 'Drifting, Controlling and Overcoming: Opiate Users who avoid becoming chronically dependent', *Journal of Drug Issues*, vol. 13, no. 2, 1983.

J. Bright and G. Petterson, *The Safe Neighbourhoods Unit* (NACRO, 1984).

G. Brown and T. Harris, *The Social Origins of Depression* (Tavistock, 1978).

I. Chein *et al.*, *The Road to H: Narcotics, delinquency and social policy* (Tavistock, 1964).

F. Davis, 'Professional Socialisation as Subjective Experience: The process of doctrinal conversion among student nurses', in H.S. Becker *et al.* (eds.), *Institutions and the Person* (Aldine, 1968).

DHSS, *Drug Misuse, Prevalence and Service Provision* (DHSS, 1985).

J. Ditton and K. Speirits, *The Rapid Increase of Heroin Addiction in Glasgow during 1981* (Univ. Glasgow, 1981).

N. Dorn and N. South, *Helping Drug Users* (Gower, 1985).

H.V. Feldman, 'Ideological Supports to Becoming and Remaining a Heroin Addict', *Journal of Health and Social Behaviour*, vol.9, 1968.

S. Fiddle, 'Sequences in Addiction', *Addictive Diseases*, vol.2, no.4, 1976.

A. Fox, *Yorkshire Report* (Hungerford Project London, 1979).

J.K. Friend *et al.*, *Alcohol-Related Problems: A study of inter-organisational relations* (Tavistock Institute of Human Relations, 1981).

H. Graham, *Women, Health and the Family* (Harvester Press, 1984).

C. Hakim, 'The Social Consequences of High Unemployment', *Journal of Social Policy*, vol.11, no.4, 1982.

R. Hartnoll, 'An Overview of Heroin and Other Drugs in Britain', paper presented to the conference on Heroin Trafficking of the Customs and Excise Group of the Society of Civil and Public Servants, London, 1984.

H.I. Hendler and R.C. Stephens, 'The Addict Odyssey: From experimentation to addiction', *International Journal of Addictions*, vol.12, no.1, 1977.

A. Henman, R. Lewis and T. Malyon, *Big Deal: The politics of the illicit drugs business* (Pluto, 1985).

Home Affairs Committee, *Misuse of Hard Drugs: Interim Report* (HMSO, 1985).

Home Office, *Crime Prevention: A coordinated approach* (Home Office, 1982).

Home Office, *Crime Prevention, An Inter-Departmental Circular*, HO 8/84 (Home Office, 1984).

E.C. Hughes, *Men and Their Work* (Free Press, 1964).

P.H. Hughes and G.A. Crawford, 'A Contagious Disease Model for Researching and Intervening in Heroin Epidemics', *Archives of General Psychiatry*, vol.27, August 1972.

P.H. Hughes *et al.*, 'The Social Structure of a Heroin Copping Community', *American Journal of Psychiatry*, vol.128, no.5, 1971.

M. Jahoda, P.F. Lazarsfield and H. Zeisel, *Marienthal: The sociography of an unemployed community* (Tavistock, 1972 edn).

M. Jahoda, *Employment and Unemployment: A social-psychological analysis* (Cambridge University Press, 1982).

A. Jamieson, A. Glanz and S. MacGregor, *Dealing with Drug Misuse* (Tavistock, 1984).

B.D. Johnson *et al.*, *Taking Care of Business: The economics of crime by heroin abusers* (Lexington, 1985).

R. Lacey and S. Woodward, *That's Life! Survey on tranquillisers* (BBC and MIND, 1985).

R. Lewis *et al.*, 'Scoring Smack: The Illicit Heroin Market in London, 1980–1983', *British Journal of Addiction*, vol.80, September 1985.

P. Marsh *et al.*, *The Rules of Disorder* (Routledge and Kegan Paul, 1978).

E. McCann, 'We Did it Ourselves! People against pushers in Dublin', *New Statesman*, 18 May 1984.

D. Musto, *The American Disease: The origins of narcotics control* (Yale University Press, 1973).

L. O'Bryan, *Adolescent Research Project: Interim Report to the DHSS* (Drug Indicators Project, 1985).

G. Pearson, 'Heroin and Unemployment', in N.H. Dorn and N. South (eds) *A Land Fit for Heroin: Drugs and Social Policy in Britain in the 1980's* (Macmillan, 1987).

H. Parker, K. Bakx and R. Newcombe, *Drug Misuse in Wirral: The First Report of the Wirral Misuse of Drugs Research Project* (University of Liverpool, 1986).

S. Peele, *The Meaning of Addiction: Compulsive experience and its interpretation* (Lexington, 1985).

J. Picardie and D. Wade, *Heroin: Chasing the dragon* (Penguin Books, 1985).

M.A. Plant, D.F. Peck and E. Samuel, *Alcohol, Drugs and School-Leavers* (Tavistock, 1985).

E. Preble and J.J. Casey, 'Taking Care of Business: The heroin user's life on the street', *International Journal of Addictions*, vol.4, no.1, 1969.

M. Rosenbaum, *Women on Heroin* (Rutgers University Press, 1981).

G.V. Stimson, *Heroin and Behaviour* (Irish University Press, 1973).

G.V. Stimson and E. Oppenheimer, *Heroin Addiction* (Tavistock, 1982).

J. Strang, 'Changing the Image of the Drug-Taker', *Health and Social Service Journal*, 11 October 1984.

A.S. Trebach, *The Heroin Solution* (Yale University Press, 1982).

N.E. Zinberg, *Drug, Set, and Setting: The basis for controlled intoxicant use* (Yale University Press, 1984).

Other Reports Consulted

B. Ashworth, *Summary of Research into the Problem of Drug Abuse in the Pendle Area of North-East Lancashire* (Blackburn Board of Social Responsibility, 1985).

A. Matthews, *Initial Impressions: Drug Abuse Research on Merseyside, May to July 1985* (Merseyside Drugs Education, Training and Research Unit, 1985).

C.J. Pattison, E.A. Barnes and A. Thorley, *South Tyneside Drug Prevalence and Indicators Study* (Centre for Alcohol and Drug Studies, St Nicholas Hospital, Newcastle upon Tyne, 1982).

D. Raistrick, G. Tober and S. Polley, *A Brief Report on Substance Misuse in Leeds* (Leeds Addiction Unit, 1984).

G. Tober, *Leeds Heroin Survey* (Leeds Addiction Unit, 1985).

P. Watson, *The Fate of Drug Addicts on a Waiting List: A Research Report* (Drugs Research Project, Prestwich Hospital, Manchester, 1985).